TECH TALK

Pre-Intermediate Workbook

John Sydes

OXFORD

UNIVERSITY PRESS

Contents

Unit 1

1 Match these jobs to their job descriptions.

a a development engineer
b a geologist
c a field service engineer
d a software programmer

e a production planner
f a quality controller
g a mechanic
h an architect

1 Works for an IT company. Writes code, updates and debugs programs. *d* ....

2 Repairs and services machines and equipment. Works for a steel producer. ....

3 Works for an oil company. Analyses rocks and minerals from the sea bed. ....

4 Works for a car producer. Checks and inspects the finished cars and writes reports. ....

5 Designs new parts and products. Works with CAD/CAM technology. Works for an aerospace company. ....

6 Works for a construction company. Is responsible for planning and designing new factories and buildings. ....

7 Works for an engineering company. Organizes and checks production schedules. ....

8 Works for a telecommunications company. Spends a lot of time travelling to companies to repair and replace or install telephone systems. ....

2 Look at these jobs and underline the activities that people normally do.

1 An architect
  a works shifts.
  b <u>negotiates prices and schedules with builders.</u>
  c <u>inspects the quality of the construction work.</u>

2 A quality controller
  a visits customers.
  b inspects samples.
  c analyses data and write reports.

3 A help desk technician
  a collects and analyses samples.
  b provides technical support.
  c spends a lot of time on the phone.

4 A warehouse manager
  a inspects new shipments.
  b checks and controls inventories.
  c writes and tests new codes.

5 An electrical engineer
  a designs circuits.
  b keeps records of inventories.
  c inspects and checks wiring and power supplies.

6 A maintenance engineer
  a repairs and maintains customers' machines.
  b replaces damaged parts.
  c produces plans and drawings.

3 Some verbs (actions) and nouns (things) have similar forms. Write the verb forms of these nouns.

1 negotiation   *negotiate* ....
2 inspection   ....
3 equipment   ....
4 specification   ....
5 maintenance   ....

6 test   ....
7 production   ....
8 construction   ....
9 security   ....
10 analysis   ....

4 Complete the sentences with the words in the list.

> negotiating inspection maintenance shifts updating
> troubleshoot shipments inventory ~~analyse~~ samples

1 I work for a pharmaceutical company. I work in the lab and I ....*analyse*.......... blood samples.

2 I'm responsible for buying new machines and equipment. I spend a lot of time .... prices and delivery times.

3 My company operates three .... The first one is from 6.00 to 14.00, the second from 14.00 to 22.00. I work the last one. It's from 22.00 to 6.00.

4 This is the quality department. This is where we do the final .... before the units are shipped to our customers.

5 We'll have to use the stairs. Our service team are doing some .... work on the lift.

6 What do I do here? Well, I .... My job is to find and correct faults in the electronic systems.

7 We don't test and examine every part. We take .... to find out what the rest is like.

8 The logistics section is responsible for checking the .... are delivered on time.

9 I'm not sure if we have 200 screens, but I'll check the .... list and call you back.

10 This is Bob. He's responsible for .... our software and security features.

5 Tick (✓) the sentences that are correct. Correct the sentences that are wrong.

            does
1 Where ~~do~~ your wife works?
2 Do you work night shifts?
3 Does your company produces electronics?
4 My brother design safety equipment.
5 That's Sheila. She tests the finished products to make sure they're OK.
6 What does these machines do?
7 I spend a lot of time on the phone. I work in technical support.
8 How long do you keeps the records?
9 Klaus and Pedro provides support to our European customers.
10 Do Pat and Maria work for an IT company?

6 Match a question or sentence on the left with a reply on the right.

1 Hello, Francesca. How are you?
2 Can I use your phone?
3 I'm afraid I can't come to your farewell party on Friday.
4 Thanks for all your help.
5 Excuse me. Do you have the time?
6 Welcome to Aero-Technologies. I'm Sally Spears.
7 Do you want me to put it here or over there?
8 Well, Mr Braun, have a good trip back.
9 Sorry I'm late.
10 Can I have another cup of tea?
11 What do you do?
12 Carlos? Can you give me a hand?

a You're welcome.
b Yes, it's almost half past one.
c Yes, of course. And help yourself to the biscuits*.
d Hello, Ali. I'm fine, thanks. And you?
e Thanks. It was nice meeting you.
f I don't mind.
g That's OK. Don't worry about it.
h Yes, of course. Go ahead.
i Sorry, Sven. I'm afraid I'm busy.
j Oh, that's a pity.
k I'm in telecommunications.
l Thanks. David Hawton. Pleased to meet you.

biscuits **BrE** – cookies **AmE**

7 Complete the questions with *Can I, Could you,* or *Would you like.*

1 ...*Can I*... borrow your pocket calculator?
2 .... hold the other end of the tape measure for me?
3 .... some more coffee?
4 .... switch the lights off if you are the last person to leave?
5 .... to order the standard or the luxury model?
6 .... use your phone?
7 .... tell me when the problem started?
8 .... give you a hand?

ALL THE COFFEE YOU CAN DRINK!

Unit 2

1 Say these letters aloud and cross out the letter with a different sound.

1 a, j, k, ~~v~~
2 b, c, h, g
3 q, w, u, z
4 d, e, t, y
5 i, l, n, s
6 g, p, r, t
7 f, j, s, x
8 l, m, n, o

2 Complete the telephone conversation with the phrases in the list.

> OK, go ahead.   No, at E-T-C dot E-S.   Can I speak to Sarah North, please?
> You're welcome.   ~~Can I help you?~~ Is there anything else?   Can I give her a message?
> Sorry, how do you spell Vazquez?   Can you speak up?

PAUL	Paul Weston, Harley Electronics. ....*Can I help you?*..........¹
PEDRO	Yes, this is Pedro Vazquez from ETC. ....²
PAUL	I'm afraid she's in a meeting. ....³
PEDRO	Yes, please. Could you ask her to email me the specifications of the JR-16 processors?
PAUL	Sorry, I didn't catch that. ....⁴
PEDRO	Yes, I need the specifications of the JR-16 processors.
PAUL	The JR-16 processors. OK. Does she have your email address, Mr Vazquez?
PEDRO	I think so, but I'll give it to you just in case she hasn't.
PAUL	...................................⁵
PEDRO	It's P underscore Vazquez at E-T-C dot E-S.
PAUL	...................................⁶
PEDRO	V-A-Z-Q-U-E-Z.
PAUL	OK, so that's P underscore Vazquez, V-A-Z-Q-U-E-Z at E-T-Z dot E-S.
PEDRO	...................................⁷
PAUL	E-T-C dot E-S.
PEDRO	Yes, that's right.
PAUL	...................................,⁸ Mr Vazquez?
PEDRO	No, that's all, thanks.
PAUL	...................................⁹ I'll give Ms North your message.
PEDRO	Thanks, bye.
PAUL	Bye.

3 Write these email and Internet addresses.

1 Paulo Santiago, one word, at H-R-C underscore ltd dot com

paulosantiago@hrc_ltd.com
....

2 G hyphen Smith nineteen eighty-five at M-U-C hyphen web dot de

....

3 Dave dot Hammerson, that's Hammer as in hammer and nail, at world hyphen online dot net

....

4 http colon, double slash, www dot science underscore world dot co dot uk

....

5 Jack dot Browne, that's B-R-O-W-N-E at Essex dot net

....

4 Match the sentences on the left with the replies on the right.

1 Can I speak to Margaret, please?   a That's S-C-H-M-I-D-T.
2 Could you speak up? The line's bad.   b Can you spell that, please?
3 Can you give me his email address?   c No, not R-I-K-A, but R-Y-K-A.
4 Are you ready?   d Yes, of course. Is that better?
5 My name's Miruto Masazumi.   e No, that's it, thanks.
6 So that's K Boborika,   f Yes, it's Tim Wilson, one word, at RT cables,
  B-O-B-O-R-I-K-A one word at ...   dot, com.
7 Anything else?   g I'm afraid she's out on a job.
8 Thanks a lot.   h No, that's Paulo underscore Silva.
9 How do you spell that?   i You're welcome.
10 Is that one word?   j Just a moment. OK, go ahead.

5 Match the imperial measurement on the left with the equivalent metric measurement on the right.

1 1 inch =   a 1.6 km
2 1 pound =   b 25.4 mm
3 1 ounce =   c 28 g
4 1 yard =   d 3.79 L
5 1 gallon =   e 454 g
6 1 foot =   f 30.48 cm
7 1 mile =   g 0.57 L
8 1 pint =   h 0.91 m

6 Read these statements. Circle T (true) or F (false).

1 A metric pound (500 g) is heavier than a US pound.   (T)/ F
2 150 km/h is slower than 100 mph.   T / F
3 An inch is shorter than a centimetre.   T / F
4 Water boils at 212 °F and freezes at 32 °F.   T / F
5 A pint of beer is more than half a litre of beer.   T / F
6 A US gallon is approximately 10 litres.   T / F
7 It will take you longer to run 100 metres than 100 yards.   T / F
8 16 ounces of gold is more expensive than 100 grams of gold.   T / F

7 Label the pictures with the words in the list.

lock   back   arm   dialling buttons   wing   keyboard
flame   ~~digital display~~   window   leg   monitor   key

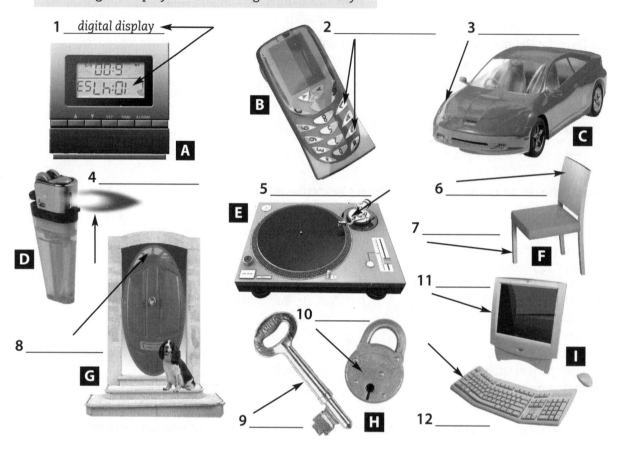

1 _digital display_

2 _____

3 _____

4 _____

5 _____

6 _____

7 _____

8 _____

9 _____

10 _____

11 _____

12 _____

8 Match these defects to the correct pictures.

1 It's too short. ....e......

2 They're upside down. ....

3 It's missing. ....

4 It's the wrong shape. .... & ....

5 It's too big and it doesn't fit. ....

6 They're in the wrong place and back to front. ....

7 It's in the wrong place. ....

8 They're missing. ....

9 Look at **8** again. What do *it* and *they* refer to?

1 _the record player arm_

2 ....

3 ....

4 ....

5 ....

6 ....

7 ....

8 ....

Unit 3

1 **Match the questions about projects on the left with the answers on the right.**

1 How much cement do you think we'll need?

2 How long will it take to install and connect the new PCs to the network?

3 Roughly how much paint do you think we'll need?

4 Approximately how much will it cost?

5 How many pumps do you think we'll need?

6 How many kilometres of cable will we need?

7 How many man-hours do you think it will take?

8 How long do you think it'll take to develop and test?

a That's difficult to say, but approximately five years.

b Well, that's hard to say. The last program took 8,000 man-hours, so let's say 5,000.

c It depends, but about three days.

d We think we'll need at least two and a half thousand.

e Well, we'll need two men for a day plus a lorry, so let's say about £600.

f About five tonnes.

g Well, the ground water is quite high here, so we'll need at least two.

h I don't think we'll need more than 50 litres.

2 **Read the conversations and underline the project they are talking about.**

1 A How far is it?
  B About five hundred kilometres.
  A So, we can ship the parts in a day.

   a delivering goods to a customer   b installing phone cables   c building a road

2 A How many tonnes do we have to transport?
  B That's difficult to say, but, roughly speaking, between four and five.
  A OK, so we'll need both the tipper trucks next week.

   a constructing a new building   b designing a new factory   c planning a new bridge

3 A Roughly how much will it cost?
  B You're looking at something like €100.
  A That's OK. And can you do it today?
  B Oh, yes. No problem. It'll be ready by 5.00.

   a designing a new engine   b equipping a laboratory   c repairing a bicycle

4 A How long do you think it'll take?
  B Approximately six months, but if the weather's bad, it'll take longer.
  A So, we won't be able to move in until September or October.

   a servicing a machine   b installing a computer network   c building a house

3 Read an email about a project and complete the sentences with *will* or *won't*.

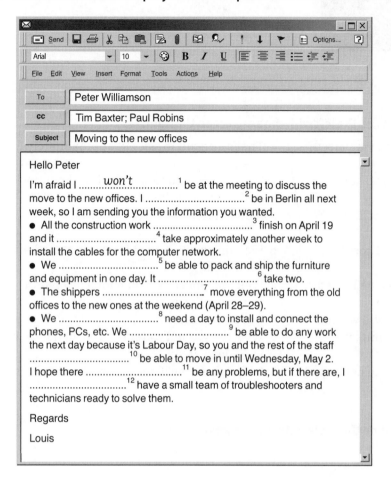

4 Complete the phrases with *How much* or *How many*.

1	*How much* .... time	5	.... information	9	.... litres
2	.... days	6	.... problems	10	.... machinery
3	.... money	7	.... euros	11	.... tools
4	.... work	8	.... data	12	.... news

5 Tick (✓) the sentences that are correct. Correct the sentences that are wrong.

1 I'll fax you the informations you wanted this afternoon.
2 How much weeks do you think you'll need to repair it?
3 The machinery is very old. I think we'll need to replace most of it.
4 The news aren't very good. It'll take about a week to get the parts we need.
5 I think it'll cost approximately five hundred euro to replace.
6 Approximately how many litres of paint do you think we'll need?
7 Roughly speaking, how much data do we need to store?
8 You're looking at something like $100,000 to buy all these equipments.
9 How much work will you have to do before it's ready?
10 We don't have many time to finish this project.

6 Read the information about these electric vehicles and complete the table of specifications.

ZAP ZAPPY ELECTRIC SCOOTER	NISSAN HYPERMINI	ESTELLE COMFORT ELECTRIC BYCYCLE

Price: €328.00	Price: Approx. €30,000	Price: €1,759
Range: ...Up to 40 km....	Range:	Range: Approx. 27 km
Weight: 16.7 kg	Weight:	Weight: 28 kg
Battery charging time:	Battery charging time: 4 hrs	Battery charging time: 2.5 hrs
Top speed:	Top speed:	Top speed: 22 km/h
Length: 104 cm	Length:	Length: 195 cm
Width: 28 cm	Width: 147.5 cm	Width: –
Height: Approx. 100 cm	Height:	Height: –
Wheels:	Wheels:	Wheels: ....

1 The cheapest of these three vehicles has a range of up to 40 km; the most expensive has a range of about 115 km.
2 It can travel the furthest, but it is also the heaviest vehicle. It weighs 840 kg.
3 The slowest vehicle has the slowest charging time, 5 hours.
4 The lightest and cheapest vehicle is slower than the other vehicles. It has a top speed of 20.8 km/h, that's 79.2 km/h slower than the fastest vehicle.
5 The Hypermini is 162.5 cm longer than the scooter and 71.5 cm longer than the electric bicycle.
6 The fastest vehicle is 55 cm higher than the scooter and 119.5 cm wider.
7 The smallest vehicle has 11-inch wheels.
8 The bicycle has the largest wheels; they are 26 inches in diameter.

7 Look at these statements and the specifications in **6**. Circle T (true) or F (false).

1 The electric bicycle is much cheaper than the electric car.　(T)/ F
2 The heaviest vehicle is also the fastest.　T / F
3 The longest vehicle is lighter than the bicycle.　T / F
4 It takes longer to charge the bike's battery than it does to charge the scooter's.　T / F
5 You can travel further with the bike's battery than you can with the scooter's.　T / F
6 The scooter is slower than the bike.　T / F
7 The bike is approximately ten times more expensive than the scooter.　T / F
8 The most expensive vehicle costs roughly 100 times more than the cheapest.　T / F

8 Use the adjectives in brackets to talk about these ways of getting from one place to another. Use a comparative (bigger, safer, more expensive) when comparing *two* things and a superlative (the biggest, the safest, the most expensive) when comparing *three* things.

1 (safe) way to travel – by train, by boat, by plane
   I think the safest way to travel is by train.
2 (convenient) for me to get to work – by bus, by car
   It's more convenient for me to get to work by car than by bus.
3 (easy) way to go down a mountain – on skis, on foot, by bike ....
4 (good) to travel around a big city – by bus, on foot ....
5 (exciting) way to cross the Sahara Desert – by camel, by balloon, by bike ....
6 (cheap) to transport a lot of large, heavy goods – by truck, by train ....
7 (interesting) to go from Moscow to Beijing – by train, by car ....
8 (expensive) to travel around my country – by train, by bus ....
9 (bad) way of getting to the nearest airport from here – by train, by bus, by car ....
10 (fun) to go – cycling, skiing ....

9 Complete the crossword.

Across

1 A packing material. It's made of air and plastic. (6, 4)
5 Another word for *lorry*. (5)
6 Another word for *approximately* or *about*. (7)
7 The things you need to do a special job. (9)
9 A number – it's more than one and less than ten. (3)
12 We use *how many* with _____ nouns, such as days, people, metres, etc. (9)
13 How much _____ you think it'll cost? (2)
14 We normally _____ the parts by road or rail. (4)
16 The _____ of the Eiffel Tower is approximately 320 metres. (6)
18 A _____ is about 3.8 litres. (6)
19 The _____ of this table are 1.60 m x 1.0 m x 0.7 m. (10)

Down

1 Good, _____, the best. (6)
2 Bad, _____, the worst. (5)
3 One or both sides of a piece of paper in a book, magazine, etc. (4)
4 _____ will it cost so much? (3)
8 Sand, cement, and bricks are all building _____. (9)
10 The noun of *wide*. (5)
11 Cars, buses, and lorries are all _____. (8)
14 The top _____ of this car is 240 km/h. (5)
15 The amount of money you have to pay to buy something. (5)
17 1,000 kg is a _____. (5)

Unit 4

1 Match the gadgets with the words in the list.

night vision binoculars   digital wrist camera   remote control   printing calculator
laser pointer   ~~gamepad~~   metal detector   electronic organizer

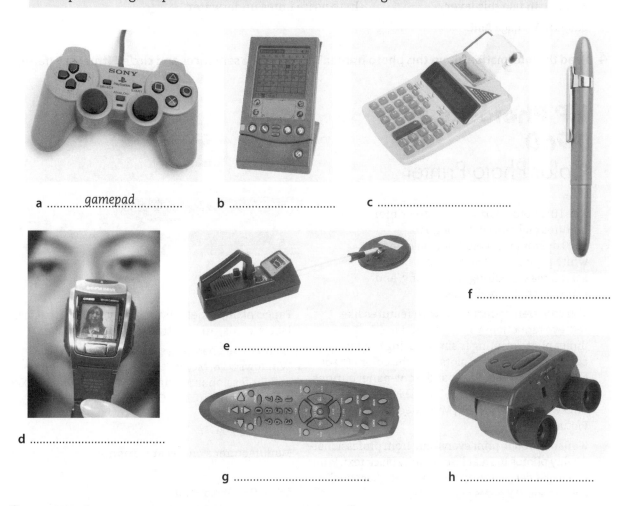

a .... *gamepad* ....   b ....   c ....

d ....

e ....

f ....

g ....   h ....

2 Read the statements and match them to the gadgets in **1**.

1 It enables you to play games on your computer. .....*a*.....
2 You can see in the dark with them. ....
3 It's for storing information such as addresses, your schedule, tasks, and notes. ....
4 It enables you to operate your television, CD, video, and amplifier. ....
5 You can find gold or silver with it. ....
6 It's for pointing at things you are talking about. ....
7 You can use it to tell the time or take pictures. ....
8 It's for doing sums. ....

3 Match the beginnings of the sentences on the left with the endings on the right.

1 This button is for ...
2 You can use this Palm program ...
3 This camera enables us ...

4 This gauge* is for ...
5 You can use this pen ...
6 This key enables you ...
7 This spanner is for ...
8 You can use this lever ...

a measuring the oil pressure.
b tightening or loosening the nuts.
c to store the names and addresses of your customers.
d to raise or lower the drill.
e to watch what is happening in this area.
f switching the machine on and off.
g to open and lock the car doors remotely.
h to write notes underwater.

gauge **BrE** – gage **AmE**

4 Read the information about this photo printer. Then read the sentences and circle T (true) or F (false).

HP Photosmart 7960
Color Photo Printer

The HP Photosmart 7960 photo printer features eight-ink color or up to 4800 dpi for great color* and black-and-white prints. The 2.5-inch color LCD screen makes editing, previewing, and printing photos really easy.

You can even correct color with features like red-eye reduction! You don't even need a PC — direct photo printing is simple using digital camera memory card slots, and the color LCD or the HP Photo Proof Sheet and front-panel buttons. Accepts CompactFlash™, SmartMedia™, Memory Stick®, Secure Digital™, MultiMediaCard, and xD-Picture Cards.

It enables you to print everything from professional-quality photos to great laser-quality black text. Print five pages per minute in normal mode (best quality color mode: 0.9 pages per minute).

Paper: plain, inkjet, photo, glossy, transparencies, labels, cards, iron-on transfers, banner paper.

Compatible operating systems: Microsoft® Windows® 98, Me, 2000 Professional, XP Home and Professional; Macintosh OS 9.1 or later, OS X v 10.1 through v 10.2 on G3 processor or greater.

Price: $229.99

Manufacturer's one-year warranty.

colour **BrE** – color **AmE**

1 You can take colour and black and white photos with it.   T / F
2 The LCD screen enables you to see the photo before you print it.   T / F
3 The red-eye reduction feature is for correcting colour.   T / F
4 You can't print photos with it if you don't have a computer.   T / F
5 The digital camera memory card slots enable you to print directly.   T / F
6 You can use any digital memory card with it.   T / F
7 It enables you to print a colour page in less than ten seconds.   T / F
8 You can print on a lot of different types of paper.   T / F
9 It's only for computers with Macintosh operating systems.   T / F
10 You can buy one for less than $230.   T / F

5 Write the opposites.

1 open   *close*   5 raise   ....

2 push   .... 6 on the left   ....

3 clockwise   .... 7 backwards   ....

4 down   .... 8 decrease   ....

6 Use the verbs in the box to complete these sentences. Use each verb once.

turn	use	~~breaks~~	increase	makes	falls	make	closes

1 If you hit an egg with a hammer, it .....*breaks*..... .

2 Water freezes when the temperature .... below 0° C.

3 A chain connecting two cogs makes both cogs .... in the same direction.

4 If you .... the pressure of the steam in a steam engine, the pistons move faster.

5 When the circuit .... , it switches on the alarm.

6 The up and down movement on the crankshaft .... the wheels turn.

7 You can lift 1,000 kg with a 1 kg weight if you .... a long enough lever.

8 How do you .... this machine work?

7 Complete the crossword.

Across

2 A wheel with 'teeth'. (3)

6 A device in a pipe or cylinder. It lets a gas or liquid move in one direction only. (5)

8 The top part of a box. You can open it. (3)

10 A: Does this cog turn anti-clockwise?
   B: _____ , it turns clockwise. (2)

11 To process old things or materials so that they can be used again. (7)

13 You can take one of these with a camera. (10)

14 The total weight that is pressing down on something. (4)

15 Part of a wheel that sticks out and turns a circular movement into an up and down movement. (3)

17 You _____ a stamp on an envelope. (5)

18 A long straight piece of wood or metal. (3)

19 A tube – gas or liquids flow through it. (4)

Down

1 A thin piece of leather or cloth that holds your trousers up. (4)

3 Cars have five or six of them, bicycles can have 21 or more. (4)

4 How _____ times a minute does this wheel rotate? (4)

5 A bar or tool you push or pull to open or lift something when you put pressure on one end of it. (5)

7 A device for opening a lock if you don't have a key. (4,4)

9 A device for making a bomb explode. (9)

12 The complete circular path that an electric current flows round. (7)

13 A wheel connected to a rope. It's for lifting things. (6)

16 To change the position of something. (4)

Unit 5

1 Complete the crossword with the Past Simple of these irregular verbs.

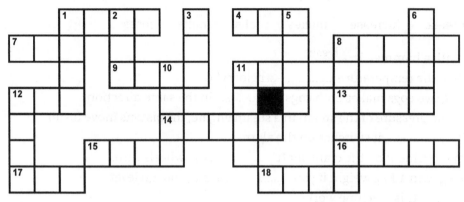

Across

1 keep	13 come
4 get	14 find
7 run	15 feel
8 begin	16 mean
9 tell	17 do
11 write	18 make
12 see	

Down

1 know	11 go
2 put	12 say
3 have	
5 take	
6 give	
8 become	
10 leave	

2 Read a story about a mining accident and the rescue. Change the verbs into the Past Simple.

On Wednesday, July 24, 2002 a team of miners (are) .....were.......¹ hard at work in Quecreek mine in Pennsylvania, USA. They (have) ....² a map so they knew that there was another older mine nearby. But they (not know) ....³ that their map was wrong and the old mine was much closer than they (think) .... .⁴

At 8.50 p.m., a terrible thing (happen) .... .⁵ Nine miners (break through) ....⁶ the connecting wall and over 500 million litres of water (pour) ....⁷ in from the old mine. They managed to escape the rushing water, but they were cut off from the surface – trapped 75 metres below ground.

The miners (try) ....⁸ to find higher ground, but it was impossible. They (find) ....⁹ a small air pocket, but the water continued to rise. The water was cold – very, very cold – and there was a limited amount of air.

Above the miners, a rescue team didn't know if they were alive or dead, but they (have to) ....¹⁰ try to reach them. They (drill) ....¹¹ a small hole to where they thought the miners were and at 5.10 a.m. they (lower) ....¹² a pipe down to the miners. Fresh, heated air (come) ....¹³ down the pipe.

So the miners (have) ....¹⁴ warm air, but the water (is) ....¹⁵ another problem. It rose and rose. Fogle, the miners' leader, (estimate) ....¹⁶ that they would all be dead in another hour. They (write) ....¹⁷ notes saying goodbye to their wives and children and (put) ....¹⁸ them in an airtight plastic bucket. The water rose to their necks, but then it (stop) ....¹⁹ The men (are) ....²⁰ still alive.

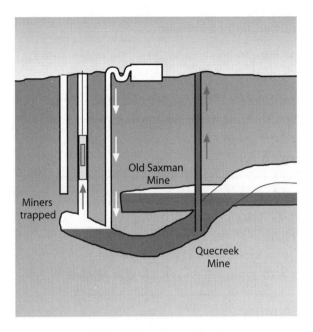

Miners trapped

Old Saxman Mine

Quecreek Mine

The rescuers on the surface (work) ....²¹ all the next day and into the night. They had to drill a tunnel to get them out. They drilled 32 metres into the ground, but at 1.50 a.m. on Friday the drill (break) ....²² They had to remove it before they (can) ....²³ continue. The rescue team (start) ....²⁴ a second rescue tunnel, 25 metres from the first. And after a 14-hour shutdown, the first rescue tunnel was back in business. But this was 43 hours from the accident now. Was it too late?

The breakthrough came on Saturday at 10.15 p.m. The first rescue drill finally (cut) ....²⁵ through to the trapped miners. 78 hours after the accident, the nine miners all escaped to safety.

Miners are the toughest people in the world. These miners were also some of the luckiest.

3 Read the story again. Circle T (true) or F (false).

1 The map the miners had didn't show the correct location of an older mine.   (T)/ F
2 The accident happened at ten to nine in the morning.   T / F
3 The miners couldn't find higher ground in time.   T / F
4 The miners' leader thought the rising water would kill them all in an hour.   T / F
5 Two rescue tunnels were started at the same time.   T / F
6 The drill broke again on Saturday at 10.15 p.m.   T / F

4 Tick (✓) the sentences that are correct. Correct the sentences that are wrong.

1 The accident ~~did~~ happened on Wednesday, July 24, 2002.
2 Did the miners have a map?
3 The miners didn't knew their map was wrong.
4 Did the rescue team know where the trapped miners was?
5 They did pumped fresh, heated air down the small hole.
6 Fogle, the miners' leader, didn't think they would live another hour.
7 When did the breakthrough came?
8 How long did it take to rescue the nine trapped miners?

5 Complete the sentences using the infinitive or the Past Simple of the verbs in brackets.

1 I ..._had_.......... (have) an accident with the car yesterday.
2 How many parts did we .... (make) last week?
3 When did you .... (see) the screws were missing?
4 I .... (tell) Chris to repair the machine last Friday.
5 The control units .... (come) yesterday.
6 Who did you .... (give) the codes to?
7 Mario and Pete .... (go) to the plant in Turin a couple of months ago.
8 We didn't .... (know) there was a problem until we .... (see) the pressure gauge.

6 Look at this page from Tim Ashton's diary. It shows his schedule for last week.

Monday
8.30 Visit supplier in Reading. Check quality of TRS11 units.
12.30 – 14.00 Quality circle meeting.

Tuesday
12.30 Presentation of last month's quality figures. Room 1036.
14.00 Phone Ken Thompson to talk about report.

Wednesday
10.00 Check installation of measuring machine. Building 045.
16.30 Take car in for service.

Thursday
9.00 TQ Meeting to discuss quality training.
10.30 Meeting with Taiwanese supplier.
12.00 Lunch with Greg at the Red Lion.
16.30 Pick up car.

Friday
8.00 Doctor
10.30 – 13.00 Meeting to discuss new packaging for finished parts
19.30 Dinner with the Swintons at Sheva's.

Saturday
Change new drill (don't forget receipt!)

Sunday
11.00 Brunch with Sophie at Castors.
19.30 Football – England v. Portugal at King's Head.

Now use the information in Tim's diary to make questions.

1 Who *did he visit on Monday morning* ....?
   He visited a supplier in Reading on Monday morning.

2 When ....?
   It was from 12.30 to 14.00 on Monday.

3 Why ....?
   He wanted to talk to him about a report.

4 What .... on Wednesday morning?
   He checked the installation of the measuring machine.

5 How many ....?
   He had three meetings on Thursday.

6 When ....?
   He went to the doctor's on Friday morning.

7 Who ....?
   He had dinner with the Swintons on Friday.

8 What ....?
   He changed his new drill on Saturday.

9 Where ....?
   He had brunch with Sophie at Castors.

10 Did ....?
    Yes, he did. He watched it at the King's Head.

7 You are the owner of a small company. Would you want these things to go up or down? Complete the table.

~~Accidents~~ Energy savings Profit Inventory Productivity Absenteeism Quality
Sales Recycled materials Material costs Emissions Downtime Wages and salaries
Waste Orders

Go up ↑	Go down ↓
	Accidents

8 Look at the table and complete the sentences using *to* or *by*.

	2nd Quarter	3rd Quarter	Percentage change
Absenteeism (Days lost)	126	119	-5.6%
Accidents	18	22	22.2%
Defects (Parts per million)	740	879	18.8%
Downtime (Hours)	98	53	-45.9%
Emissions (Tonnes CO_2)	176	195	10.8%
Inventory (US$)	89,653	76,592	-14.6%
Productivity	10.37	10.14	-2.2%
Recycled materials (Tonnes)	493	506	2.6%
Waste (Tonnes)	769	747	-2.9%

1 The number of accidents went up ...by.... 22% in the third quarter.
2 Productivity decreased .... 10.14. That's a decrease of 2.2%.
3 We recycled 493 tonnes of materials in the second quarter. This rose .... 506 in the third quarter.
4 Downtime fell .... 45.9% .... 53 hours.
5 We managed to reduce the amount of waste we produce .... 22 tonnes.
6 The number of days lost went down .... 119. Absenteeism fell .... 5.6%.
7 CO_2 emissions increased .... 19 tonnes. That's a rise of more than 10%.
8 We reduced the inventory .... nearly 15%. It fell .... $76,592.

Unit 6

1 Match the problems on the left with ideas and questions on the right.

1 I'm not getting my emails.

2 My car doesn't start when it's cold.

3 It's really difficult to turn this key.

4 I can't get a signal on my mobile.

5 My PC crashes when I scan in a photo.

6 The loudspeaker on the left doesn't work.

7 I get a really fuzzy picture on CNN.

8 I don't know what's wrong, but I can't make a hole in this metal.

a It could be a memory problem.

b What happens when you go outside the building?

c It might be the battery.

d What happens when you reverse the direction the drill's turning in?

e Have you checked if your mailbox is full?

f What happens when you change channels?

g Have you tried oiling the lock?

h Have you checked the cable is connected properly?

2 Complete the text with the words in the list.

problem help ~~work~~ take out dry check cleaning empty connected
blocked function come out cleaned manual wrong

How to solve your printer problems

Problem	Possible fixes
The printer doesn't __work__.[1]	_____[2] the power is on. Make sure the printer cable is _____.[3] The printer might be jammed. Open the printer and remove all the jammed paper – make sure you get all the pieces out. If you use a network printer, it could be a network _____.[4]
Paper feed problems (no paper or too much paper goes through the printer) paper	The printer could be jammed. Open the printer's covers and _____[5] all the jammed paper. The printer's rollers might be _____.[6] When this happens several sheets of often _____[7] at the same time. Use a special liquid for _____[8] the rollers if this doesn't _____,[9] call a service technician.
The printer prints out the _____[10] colours.	Open the printer and check that the printer cartridges still have ink in them. Printers use different colour cartridges and mixes the ink in them to make colours. If one cartridge is _____,[11] the colours will be wrong. Most inkjet printers have a self-cleaning _____.[12] Check the _____[13] for the correct self-cleaning program. One of the print cartridges or the print head could be _____[14] with old ink. They can be _____[15] with alcohol, but it is usually easier to buy a new colour cartridge.

3 **Underline what can go wrong with these things.**

1 There's a problem with one of the hot water pipes. It's …
   a <u>blocked</u>   b <u>leaking</u>   c burnt out

2 The batteries in this radio are …
   a empty   b flat   c leaking

3 Most of the bolts on the bike were …
   a blunt   b loose   c rusty

4 I'm not 100% sure what the problem with this electric pump is, but it might be …
   a jammed   b burnt out   c flat

5 The old fuel tanks in building 6.1 are …
   a empty   b stiff   c rusty

6 I can't open this door. It might be …
   a jammed   b blocked   c torn

4 **Match the problem on the left with a way to fix it on the right.**

1 The monitor's dirty.   a OK, I'll replace it.

2 I think they're flat.   b Yes, I know. It needs repairing.

3 These screws are loose.   c They need recharging.

4 The bulb has burnt out.   d Do you want me to sharpen it?

5 This knife is blunt.   e Are they? OK, I'll fill them.

6 I can't move this lever. It's so stiff.   f It needs cleaning.

7 This pipe's leaking.   g Yes, I know. I think it needs oiling.

8 These cans are all empty.   h Can you tighten them for me?

5 **Number the sentences in the conversation.**

.... HARRY   I'm not sure, but it might be the cooling fan. It's making a funny noise. I think the belt is slipping. Can you fix it?

.... KEN   I'll be right over. I'll be with you five minutes.

...1... HARRY   Ken, this is Harry. What are you doing?

.... HARRY   Great! Thanks a lot, Ken.

.... KEN   What's wrong with it?

.... HARRY   How soon can you get here?

.... KEN   Yes, if it's the belt, I can replace it in twenty minutes or so, but if there's a problem with the fan, it might take longer to fix.

.... HARRY   We've got a problem with one of the machines in the workshop.

.... KEN   Hello, Harry. I'm repairing that electric motor you asked me to. Why? What's up?

6 Match the list of verbs and things to the pictures.

1 .....*d*.... + ...*n*....

2 .... + ...

3 .... + ...

4 .... + ...

5 .... + ...

6 .... + ...

7 .... + ...

8 .... + ...

Verbs		**Things**	
a	run	i	a tomato
b	repair	j	a hole / the ice
c	fill	k	a test
d	~~hammer~~	l	power lines
e	construct	m	a car / petrol
f	drill	n	~~a nail / wood~~
g	cut	o	a car
h	spray	p	a building

7 Look at the pictures in **6**. Use the verbs and things to write about what the people are doing in these pictures.

1 *He's hammering a nail into some wood.*
....

2 ....

3 ....

4 ....

5 ....

6 ....

7 ....

8 ....

Unit 7

1 Complete the questions using the words in the list.

| What | Where | When | Why | Who | Which | How |

1 _When_ does the meeting start?
   At 11.30, I think.

2 .... are you staying?
   At the Maddison Hotel.

3 .... PC do you think we should buy?
   Hmm, that one looks very good.

4 .... do you come to work?
   By bus.

5 .... did you speak to?
   José Fernandez.

6 .... does that machine produce?
   Plastic screws.

7 .... don't we buy a new one?
   Because it's too expensive.

8 .... do you normally finish work?
   Around 4.00 p.m.

9 .... is your boss?
   Keith Winters. Do you know him?

10 .... does USB stand for?
    Universal Serial Bus, I think.

11 .... is your car parked?
    It's next to the canteen.

12 .... model would you like?
    The ADC 51-33.

2 Complete the questions using the words in the list.

| kind of | often | long | size | much | ~~time~~ | many | colour |

1 What _time_ do you start work in the morning?

2 How .... is a mile?

3 What .... work do you do?

4 How .... does this virus program cost?

5 What .... is the live wire? Blue or brown?

6 How .... units can we produce in an hour?

7 What .... LCD screen do you need? 14- or 17-inch?

8 How .... should I change the oil?

3 Underline the correct word.

1 30 litres of petrol _last_/take me about two weeks.
2 How long do you think it will last/take to complete the building work?
3 These batteries are both flat! They didn't last/take very long.
4 How long do you think the strike will last/take?
5 It might last/take another six weeks to get the parts we need.
6 It lasted/took me nearly an hour to get to work this morning. The traffic was terrible.
7 I've ordered 1,000 packets of paper for the photocopiers. That should last/take us a couple of months.
8 How long will it last/take to repair the machines?

4 Complete the email with *in*, *on*, or *at*.

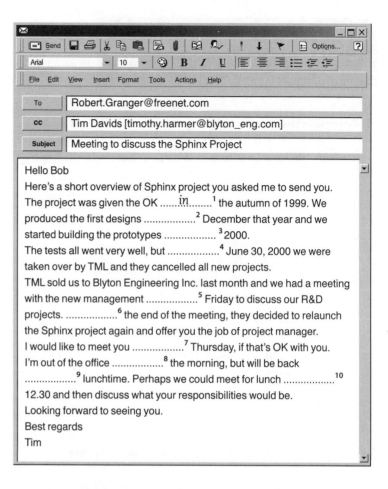

To Robert.Granger@freenet.com

cc Tim Davids [timothy.harmer@blyton_eng.com]

Subject Meeting to discuss the Sphinx Project

Hello Bob

Here's a short overview of Sphinx project you asked me to send you. The project was given the OK ....in........[1] the autumn of 1999. We produced the first designs ....[2] December that year and we started building the prototypes ....[3] 2000.

The tests all went very well, but ....[4] June 30, 2000 we were taken over by TML and they cancelled all new projects.

TML sold us to Blyton Engineering Inc. last month and we had a meeting with the new management ....[5] Friday to discuss our R&D projects. ....[6] the end of the meeting, they decided to relaunch the Sphinx project again and offer you the job of project manager.

I would like to meet you ....[7] Thursday, if that's OK with you. I'm out of the office ....[8] the morning, but will be back ....[9] lunchtime. Perhaps we could meet for lunch ....[10] 12.30 and then discuss what your responsibilities would be.

Looking forward to seeing you.

Best regards

Tim

5 Write these numbers.

1 one thousand nine hundred and ninety-nine .....1,999.....

2 a billion ....

3 a million square metres ....

4 a trillion ....

5 nineteen ninety nine ....

6 a hundred thousand cubic metres ....

7 a hundred million ....

8 one point nine, nine, nine ....

6 Circle the number you think is correct.

1 The average bed contains .... of mites (mites are very small insects).
   a hundreds   b thousands   ⓒ millions   d billions

2 Britons consume over .... litres of mineral water a year.
   a 100 thousand   b 10 million   c a billion   d a trillion

3 The population of the world is approximately ....
   a 650 million   b 6.5 billion   c 65 billion   d 650 billion.

4 Worldwide consumption of oil is around .... tonnes a year.
   a 3.5 billion   b 35 billion   c 350 billion   d 3.5 trillion

5 About .... motor vehicles were produced in 2002.
   a 6 million   b 60 million   c 600 million   d 6 billion

6 There are about .... people per square kilometre in Monaco.
   a 170   b 1,700   c 17,000   d 170,000

7 .... PCs have been sold since 1985.
  a 10 million   b 100 million   c 1 billion   d 10 billion

8 The temperature at the centre of the Earth is estimated to be ....
  a 555 °C   b 1,500 °C   c 5,500 °C   d 25,500 °C

7 Complete the text using the numbers in the list.

4,000 km   ~~ten thousand times~~   35 cm   75%   hundreds of thousands   75,000 years   21 °

A super volcano can explode with a force .ten.thousand.times.....¹ greater than a normal volcano. They 'sleep' for ....² of years, slowly building up a huge reservoir of magma – hot, liquid rock. When super volcanoes do erupt, the force of the explosion is so powerful that it can destroy continents and kill most forms of life on this planet.

The last eruption of a super volcano was in Toba, Sumatra, ...³ ago. It had 10,000 times the explosive force of Mount St Helens. Thousands of cubic kilometres of ash were thrown into the atmosphere and it blocked out the sun all over the world. ....⁴ away, ...⁵ of ash covered the ground killing ....⁶ of all plants in the northern hemisphere. Global temperatures fell by ....⁷ overnight.

a few thousand   600,000 years   50 km   1,000 km   billions   74 cm higher
85 km x 45 km   1,000 km³   12.5 cm

The largest super volcano in the world is in Yellowstone Park in the USA. It is ....⁸ The ground in Yellowstone Park is ....⁹ than it was in 1923 – which means the magma reservoir under the park is growing quickly. The volcano erupts every ....¹⁰ and the last eruption was 640,000 years ago. So scientists think there will be another eruption soon.

What will happen if it does erupt? Magma would be thrown ....¹¹ into the air. All life within ....¹² of Yellowstone would be destroyed by the explosion and falling lava. Volcanic ash could cover places as far away as Iowa and the Gulf of Mexico. ....¹³ of lava would pour out of the volcano – that's enough to cover the whole of the USA in a ....¹⁴ thick layer of lava.

The Sumatra explosion reduced the population of the world to ....¹⁵ and scientists believe the same thing could happen again when the volcano under Yellowstone Park finally explodes. This time ....¹⁶ of human lives would be at risk.

Unit 8

1 Look at these instructions about installing and using a photocopying machine. Then read the sentences and circle T (true) or F (false).

1	You have to install the copier in a place that is hot and sunny.	T / (F)
2	You mustn't look at the exposure lamp when you're using the copier.	T / F
3	You must place the copier near a heater.	T / F
4	You mustn't drop paper clips into the machine.	T / F
5	You need to open the front panel when copying.	T / F
6	You don't need to worry about putting the copier in a dusty area.	T / F
7	You have to install the copier in a place that gets fresh air.	T / F
8	You mustn't put the copier in a place where the temperature is lower than 10 °C.	T / F

2 Underline the correct verb to complete these operating instructions.

1 You *must/mustn't* copy originals that are glued or stuck together.
2 If there is a paper jam, you *don't have to/have to* open the copier to remove the paper.
3 You *mustn't/don't have to* store the toner in a damp or wet place.
4 You *don't have to/must* switch the copier off before removing the covers and putting your hand inside the machine.
5 You *mustn't/need to* pull out the plug when you are copying something.
6 You *don't have to/mustn't* cut the wire when the copier is plugged in.
7 You *don't have to/mustn't* call a service technician when there is a paper jam.
8 You *needn't/mustn't* put drinks on the copier.
9 You *have to/needn't* select the number of copies you want before pressing the start button.
10 You *mustn't/needn't* sort the copies if you select the sort function.

3 Read the statements. Which object do they refer to?

a saw   b four-stroke engine   c hoist   d bicycle

1 It has a blade, a handle, and teeth. ....*a*....

2 It's for raising or lowering heavy things. ....

3 It has a crank, a chain, and two pedals. ....

4 It moves up and down and changes the up and down movement into a circular one. ....

5 It has hooks and a level. ....

6 If you move it backwards and forwards, it cuts. ....

7 It has cams, valves, and pistons. ....

8 If you turn the front gears clockwise, it rotates the rear wheel clockwise. ....

4 Underline the correct verb.

1 A The machines will weigh just over 40 tonnes.

   B Well, then the floor will need ...

      a lowering   b <u>strengthening</u>   c reversing   d shortening

2 A We have to design a clock for the Bavarian tourist board. They
      want one that goes backwards.

   B Backwards? Well, the cogs and the mechanism need ...

      a lowering   b repositioning   c raising   d reversing

3 A The temperature in the refrigeration unit is -3 °C.

   B Oh, it should be -10 °C. So, it needs ...

      a raising   b lowering   c lengthening   d repositioning

4 A I think some of these keys are in the wrong place. The function
      keys should be on the top of the keyboard, not at the bottom.

   B Yes, you're right! They need ...

      a repositioning   b raising   c shortening   d reversing

5 We have a problem here. If bigger planes want to land at our airport, the runway needs ...

   a reversing   b raising   c lengthening   d lowering

6 A Ouch! I keep banging my head on this light!

   B I know. I have the same problem and I'm a bit shorter than you. It needs ...

      a raising   b lowering   c shortening   d lengthening

5 Read the dialogue about the invention below and match the words in the list with the correct items 1–12 in the picture.

A Hey, what's that?

B That's my new invention for keeping fit when I watch television. If there aren't any good films on, I can also keep fit by reading a book.

A How does it work?

B Well, the bicycle's on rollers and it's held in place by the support, so I can't fall off …

A Isn't the support in the wrong place? I think you should move it nearer the handlebars.

B Good idea. Yes, I'll reposition it.

A And what's all that wire for?

B Yes, there's too much wire. It needs shortening. The wire supplies the television with electricity. It goes from the dynamo to the switch on the handlebars and then into the back of the television.

A But that won't work!

B Huh? Why not?

A Because the front wheel doesn't turn round when you pedal, so it can't turn the dynamo.

B Oh …

electric wire
dynamo
saddle
handlebars
screen
on/off switch
gears
support
crank
remote control unit
rollers
book holder

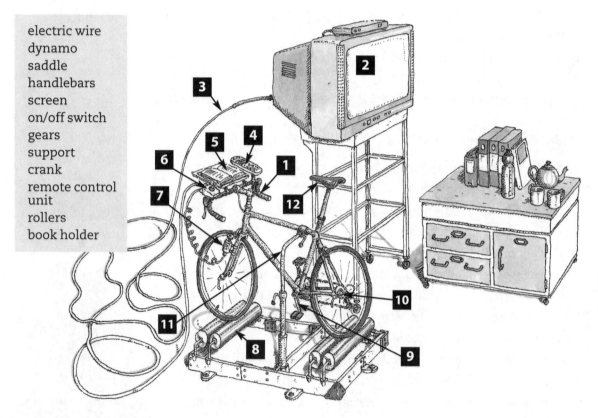

6 Circle T (true) or F (false).

1 The saddle needs lowering.   (T)/ F
2 The wire needs lengthening.   T / F
3 It's for keeping fit when you watch television.   T / F
4 The television needs repositioning.   T / F
5 There's an on/off switch and a remote control unit on the support.   T / F
6 If there's nothing interesting on television, the user can keep fit and read a book.   T / F
7 This idea won't work because there's nothing to support the bike.   T / F
8 This idea won't work because the front wheel doesn't turn.   T / F

7 Underline the objects that could be damaged.

1 It's bent.
   a <u>a nail</u>   b <u>a pipe</u>   c <u>an aerial</u>   d paint
2 It's chipped.
   a paint   b a tooth   c a can   d a cup
3 It's corroded.
   a a rope   b a battery   c a pipe   d a car body
4 It's cracked.
   a an egg   b a wall   c a glass   d a carpet
5 It's crushed.
   a a car   b a can   c a box   d a rope
6 It's dented.
   a a bucket   b a gold cup   c a car body   d a tyre
7 It's dusty.
   a water   b the air   c a file   d a PC monitor
8 It's frayed.
   a a rope   b a CD   c a carpet   d a shirt
9 It's scratched.
   a a CD   b an arm   c a carpet   d a glass
10 It's worn.
   a a monitor   b a shoe   c a carpet   d a tooth

8 Look at the cartoon and circle T (true) or F (false).

1   The flag is frayed   Ⓣ/ F
2   One of the windows is dirty. T / F
3   The tyres are chipped.   T / F
4   The aerial is bent.   T / F
5   The front of the car is
    cracked.   T / F
6   The body of the car is dirty
    and corroded.   T / F

Unit 9

a

b

DANGER
Overhead
cables

c

WARNING
Keep cover closed
while running

1 Look at these warning signs and match them with the hazards below.

1 Slipping and falling ....*g*....

2 Damaging your hearing ....

3 Electric shocks ....

4 Laser radiation ....

5 Crushing parts of your body in moving machinery ....

6 Clothing getting caught in machinery ....

7 Poisoning or burning ....

8 Injuring your head or feet ....

d

HARD HATS AND SAFETY
BOOTS MUST BE WORN
ON THIS SITE

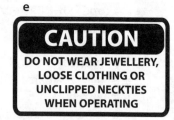
e

CAUTION
DO NOT WEAR JEWELLERY,
LOOSE CLOTHING OR
UNCLIPPED NECKTIES
WHEN OPERATING

f

DANGER
Wear goggles and
rubber gloves when
handling chemicals

h

Ear protection area

g

CAUTION
WET FLOOR

Cleaning in
progress

2 Complete the conversations using *should*, *shouldn't*, or *could*.

1 A You ....*shouldn't*....¹ use a ladder here. You ....² get electrocuted.

   B Yes, I know, but I need to change that light bulb. I can't reach it without a ladder.

   A OK, but switch the electricity off first.

2 A Why aren't you wearing safety glasses? You ....³ get some of that stuff in your eyes!

   B Yes, I know I ....⁴ be wearing them, but I can't find them. Can I borrow yours?

3 A You ....⁵ wear ear-defenders.

   B Sorry? It's so noisy in here, I didn't understand what you said.

   A I said you ....⁶ work in here without ear-defenders!

4 A You ....⁷ lose your hand in that machine. You ....⁸ operate it without the safety cover on.

   B I can't get the cover on. The screws are missing.

   A Well, you ....⁹ switch the machine off and phone someone in the maintenance department before you have an accident.

5 A Hey! Be careful! The floor's wet. You ....¹⁰ slip and break an arm or a leg.

   B Well, you ....¹¹ put a sign up then.

   A I have put a sign up! Maybe you ....¹² open your eyes and read it!

3 Number these instructions for installing a sound card in a PC.

_____ **a** Restart your computer and turn the speakers on.

_____ **b** You need to insert the sound card gently but firmly into the slot. You can move the card backwards and forwards to get it into position if necessary, but make sure you don't force it in. Don't touch any connectors on the card.

_____ **c** Static electricity can seriously damage the sound card and the motherboard. You should ground yourself to your computer. You can ground yourself by touching a metal part of the PC chassis.

_____ **d** If your operating system finds the sound card on startup, follow the instructions to install the card's driver and additional software. If the operating system doesn't find the sound card, manually complete the installation using the 'Add New Hardware' control panel.

__1__ **e** Shut down your computer, disconnect all peripherals (the monitor, keyboard, and mouse, etc.), and remove the cover.

_____ **f** Now, reconnect the monitor, keyboard, and mouse. Don't forget to connect speakers to the sound card's ports.

_____ **g** Connect the cables from the CD-ROM or DVD-ROM drive to the new sound card.

_____ **h** Remove the old sound card, if there is one. Put the new sound card into that slot if it fits. If your computer doesn't have a sound card, find a free PCI slot.

_____ **i** Finally, you need to test your sound card by playing a music CD. If it plays OK, shut down the computer again and replace the cover.

__6__ **j** You need to screw the sound card into the slot holder, if it has a screw hole.

4 Which steps in **3** do these pictures show?

a ....4....

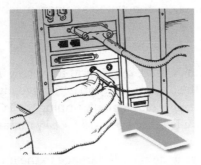

b ....

c ....

d ....

e ....

f ....

5 Refer to the instructions in **3** again and circle T (true) or F (false).

1 Before installing the card, you should shut down the PC and disconnect the peripherals. (T)/ F
2 You should ground yourself. You could be seriously injured by an electric shock. T / F
3 You should leave the old sound card in the PC and put the new sound card into a free slot. T / F
4 You shouldn't use force when inserting the card. You should insert it gently, but firmly. T / F
5 The cables from the CD- and/or DVD-ROM drives should be connected to the sound card. T / F
6 If your operating system can't find the sound card, you should install the drivers manually. T / F
7 You should shut down the PC and replace the cover before you test the sound card. T / F
8 To test the sound card you should put a data CD in the CD- or DVD-ROM drive. T / F

6 Write the adverbs.

1 bad   *badly*   5 hard   ....
2 tight   ....   6 easy   ....
3 good   ....   7 fast   ....
4 slow   ....   8 complete ....

7 Now use the adverbs in **6** to complete these sentences. Use each word once.

1 Make sure the nuts are done up ...*tightly*....
2 This phone was .... designed. It's really difficult to change the batteries.
3 We need the spare parts .... In fact, we need them by tomorrow.
4 Don't hit it too ....! You could break it.
5 This machine works really .... The old one was useless.
6 The number of units we sell has fallen .... from 100,000 in 2000 to 97,000 last year.
7 The program can .... be downloaded from the Internet.
8 The workshop has been .... renovated and new machinery installed.

8 Underline the correct word.

1 You can install a card in your PC quick/<u>quickly</u> and easy/<u>easily</u> if you follow these instructions.
2 It's a good/well idea to have the drivers and instructions ready before you start.
3 Before you remove the cover, physical/physically unplug the PC from the socket.
4 When you open the case, you'll either see a solid/solidly metal wall, or an open bay full of wires and circuit boards.
5 Static electricity can cause serious/seriously damage to the motherboard.
6 Don't use force if the cable doesn't disconnect easy/easily.
7 The old card may need one or two gentle/gently pulls to come loose.
8 It is easy/easily to misalign a card, so check carefully/carefully that it is proper/properly aligned in the slot.

1 Use the words in the list to describe these shapes.

cone   square   triangle   oval   semi-circle   ~~cube~~   sphere   cylinder   circle   rectangle

1 ....*cube*....

2 ....

3 ....

4 ....

5 ....

6 ....

7 ....

8 ....

9 ....

10 ....

2 Complete the list of nouns and adjectives.

Noun	Adjective
1 circle	*circular* .... or round
2	semi-circular
3 square	....
4 triangle	....
5	cylindrical
6 cone	....
7 sphere	....
8	cubic
9 rectangle	....
10 oval	....

3 What shape are these things? Label the pictures with the words in the list.

1 _heart-shaped_   2 ....   3 ....   4 ....

5 ....   6 ....   7 ....   8 ....

T-shaped
X-shaped
~~heart-shaped~~
S-shaped
star-shaped
Y-shaped
U-shaped
L-shaped

4 Read this description of a building and complete the picture.

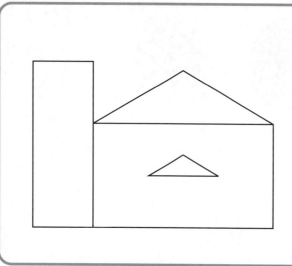

There is a rectangular door at the bottom of the tower. There's an oval window in the middle of the tower and a circular window at the top. The roof of the tower is dome-shaped. On the left of the tower, there is a spherical bush. It's as high as the rectangular door.

There's a rectangular door under the small triangular roof. It has a heart-shaped window in it.

On either side of the door there are two cubes. There are two cylinders between the cubes and the small triangular roof. The cubes and the cylinders support the small triangular roof.

There are two square windows on either side of the door and above them are two semi-circular windows.

There is also a semi-circular window in the middle of the roof.

There is a conical tree on the right-hand side of the house. It's as high as the top of the roof.

5 Decide what these things are. Underline the best answer.

1 A screwdriver
a gadget   b appliance   **c** _tool_   d machine

2 A microscope
a implement   b instrument   c gadget   d appliance

3 An electric toaster
a tool   b gadget   c appliance   d machine

4 A video-watch
a gadget   b tool   c instrument   d appliance

5 A spanner
a instrument   b machine   c implement   d tool

6 A potato peeler
a appliance   b instrument   c implement   d machine

7 A voltmeter
a instrument   b machine   c appliance   d implement

8 Digital speaking clock
a instrument   b gadget   c tool   d machine

6 Write the words in the list in the correct column.

Colours	Materials	Shapes	Tools / Machines
	steel		

~~steel~~ sphere purple scissors pink cube plastic wrench yellow copper rectangle calculator titanium saw cotton control unit cone rubber green aluminium oval pump quartz cylinder

7 Complete the crossword.

Across

1 The colour you get when you mix blue, red, and yellow together. (5)
5 A hammer isn't a machine, it's a _____ . (4)
7 Is this screw _____ of steel? (4)
8 Red and yellow = _____ (6)
11 If a shape has six square sides of the same size, it is _____ . (5)
12 An implement. It is used in the garden to make holes in the ground. (5)
14 It's round at the bottom and pointed at the top. (4)
16 Another word for *circular*. (5)
17 A: They want 100,000 by next Tuesday.
   B: 100,000! That's a _____ . (3)
18 A round object shaped like a ball. (6)
20 The colour you get when you mix black with white. (4)
21 When you put something together with something else to increase the size, number, or value. For example, if you _____ 3 to 6, you get 9. (3)
22 It's round. It's made of glass. Cameras, magnifying glasses, and microscopes have one or more of them. (4)
23 The colour of grass. (5)
24 *Steel, wood, plastic*, and *rubber* are all _____ . (9)
25 The abbreviation for *millilitres*. (2)

Down

2 The opposite of *black*. (5)
3 Do you want it made in gold _____ silver? (2)
4 How many colours can you see _____ this picture? (2)
6 The shape of a long, but thin circle. (4)
7 This _____ produces bottles and that _____ wraps them. (7)
9 A modern device that is not really needed, but is nice to have. (6)
10 *Gold, silver,* and *steel* are _____ . (6)
12 The human eye cannot _____ infra-red light. (3)
13 ._____ you want to paint this room white or yellow? (2)
15 An electronic form of sending messages from one computer to another. (1-4)
16 A colour that is often used in warning signs. (3)
19 The past tense of *run*. (3)

Unit 11

1 **Read the dialogue and circle T (true) or F (false).**

A So, what kind of tests do you do on motorcycle helmets?
B Well, first we do a roll-off test.
A A roll-off test? What's that?
B It's a special test to see if the helmet could come off your head in an accident.
A OK, then what?
B Then we do some impact tests. In the first impact test, we drop the helmet from a height of two metres at a speed of 20 km/h and measure the shock-absorption.
A Shock-absorption?
B Yes, a helmet must be able to absorb and reduce the shock when it hits the ground. We do that four times – twice to the front of the helmet and twice to one side. The shock mustn't be more than 200 g for longer than two milliseconds.
A OK, do you do any other kinds of test?
B Yes, we do a chin bar test. The chin bar is the part of helmet below your mouth. We test to see how strong they are. About 20% of the helmets fail this test.
A Really? That's a lot. Could you test my crash helmet to see if it's safe?
B Yes, of course we could ... but you'd have to buy a new helmet afterwards.
A But what if it passes?
B Even if it passes the tests, it would be too badly damaged to be safe to wear again.

1 The first test that is done is the roll-off test.	Ⓣ/ F
2 Several impact tests are done to different parts of the helmet.	T / F
3 The shock is measured in grams per second.	T / F
4 Five different impact tests are carried out.	T / F
5 The helmets are passed as safe if the shock measured is more than 200 g for longer than 2 milliseconds.	T / F
6 The last test to be done is the chin bar test.	T / F
7 About 20% of the helmets are failed after this test.	T / F
8 The helmets that are tested are all badly damaged by the tests.	T / F

2 **Read the sentences and decide if they are active (A) or passive (P).**

1 This is where the crash tests are carried out. ....P....

2 We use crash-test dummies to measure the injuries. ....

3 A 1,360 kg barrier is driven into the side of a car at 50 km/h. ....

4 Side air bags can prevent a lot of serious head injuries. ....

5 But a lot of side air bags are not designed to protect smaller passengers. ....

6 We now use smaller dummies in a lot of our tests. ....

7 These tests are very expensive to set up and carry out, but they can save a lot of lives. ....

8 Over 40,000 people a year are killed in traffic accidents in the USA. ....

3 Use the verb *be* and the past participle of the verb in brackets to change these active sentences into the passive.

1 First, we take some blood samples.

First, some blood samples (take) ......*are taken*........ .

2 They write the safety standard number on the back.

The safety standard number (write) .... on the back.

3 We do all the trials in the lab over there.

All the trials (do) .... in the lab over there.

4 We give the samples to independent research institutes.

The samples (give) .... to independent research institutes.

5 Before we make any decision, we need to know how the field trials go.

Before any decision (make) .... , we need to know how the field trials go.

4 Look at these inventions and complete the sentences using the words in the list.

| It's for (x2)   It has (x3)   Rotate   Use this   This keeps |

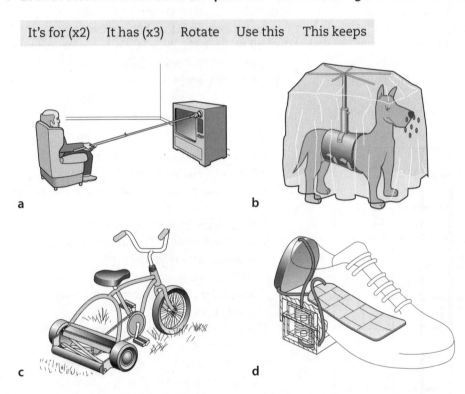

a   b

c   d

1 ......*It has*.......... holes in the front to stop the umbrella from fogging up.

2 .... to change channels on your television.

3 .... a compressor and heat exchangers built into the heel.

4 .... keeping your feet cool on hot days.

5 .... the pedals to turn the blades at the back and move forwards.

6 .... an adjustable arm.

7 .... taking your best friend for a walk in the rain.

8 .... your grass cut short.

5 Look at the inventions in **4** again and say which device(s) has / have these things.

1 a rubber cushion and tubes ....*d*....
2 two straps at the bottom and a frame at the top ....
3 a clamp at one end of it for rotating buttons and knobs ....
4 a plastic cover ....
5 a gear, rollers, and a chain ....
6 gas and pipes in it ....
7 an adjustable arm ....
8 lots of rotating parts ....

6 Match these two-part instructions for the inventions in **4**.

1 Sit on the saddle and pedal
2 Change the channel
3 Make sure the holes are at the front
4 All you need to do is walk
5 Do up the two straps
6 Adjust the length of the arm
7 Rotate the blades
8 Put the rubber cushion into the shoe

a to ensure it doesn't fog up.
b to pump the gas around it.
c by turning the arm.
d before putting your foot into it.
e before using it for the first time.
f by turning the pedals.
g to fasten the umbrella to the dog.
h to cut the grass.

7 Complete the puzzle.

1 Either something passes a test, or it _____ .
2 The past participle of the verb *begin*.
3 Another expression for *to begin to burn* is *to catch on* _____ .
4 The past participle of the verb *leave*.
5 A specimen or small quantity of something that shows what the rest is like.
6 These parts are _____ in Germany.
7 A bright burning gas that comes from something that is on fire.
8 These tests are used to _____ how strong the materials are.
9 This drug has to _____ clinically tested before it is sold to the public.
10 In the crease test a lot of pressure is _____ to the ties.
11 A tie is something you wear around your _____ .

Unit 12

1 Match the signs with the places you could see them.

a   b   c   d   e   f   g   h

1 In an aeroplane ...*b*...

2 In a shopping centre or car park ....

3 On a packet or parcel ....

4 On a machine ....

5 At an airport or station ....

6 At a petrol station ....

7 In a tall building ....

8 At the roadside ....

2 Look at the signs in **1** again. Say which sign means:

1 unplug the machine. ...*a*...

2 fragile, handle with care. ....

3 don't use the lift when there's a fire. ....

4 you are being watched by closed circuit television cameras. ....

5 only fast-moving vehicles are allowed on this road. ....

6 you can only stop for a few minutes to unload bags. ....

7 a flame or cigarette could cause an explosion or a fire. ....

8 safety belts must be worn. ....

3 Match a warning on the left with a product on the right.

1 Caution! Avoid eye contact.

2 Best before – see bottom of can.

3 Fragile! Do not drop!

4 Do not attempt to stop the blade with your hand.

5 Do not put metal objects inside.

6 Smoking can kill.

7 Important! Keep your PIN secret at all times.

8 Objects in the mirror are closer than they appear.

9 Do not recharge or put in backwards.

10 Warning! May cause drowsiness. Do not drive or operate dangerous machinery.

a Glass teapot

b Microwave oven

c Packet of cigarettes

d Car

e Tin of frankfurters

f Battery

g Sleeping tablets

h Credit card

i Spray paint

j Electric saw

4 Here are some silly warning signs. Use the phrases in the list to complete these warnings.

> are sharp   will be prosecuted   ~~with remaining eye~~   Warning: misuse may   for drying pets
> cancer in laboratory mice!   For indoor   actually behind you

1 Do not look into the laser .....*with remaining eye*..... . (on a laser pen).

2 Do not use .... (on a microwave oven)

3 Remember, objects in the mirror are .... (on a rear-view mirror)

4 Warning: knives .... ! (on the packaging of a stone for sharpening knives)

5 Warning: can cause .... (on a box of rat poison)

6 .... or outdoor use only. (on a string of Christmas lights)

7 Danger! Touching these wires means instant death. Anyone found doing so
.... (on a sign at a railway station)

8 .... cause injury or death. (on the barrel of a .22 calibre gun)

5 Match a suggestion on the left with a response on the right.

1 How about renting some storage space?

2 I think we should buy these parts from India.

3 What we need is a third shift.

4 Couldn't we use more plastic to make the bodies?

5 How about buying recycled paper?

6 Why don't we open an office in London?

7 What we need is some laser drills.

8 How about putting a warning sign on them? "Do not eat!"

a Yes, but don't forget it takes about 30 days to ship them to Hamburg.

b Yes, why not? It would help cut our printing costs.

c Maybe, but it's not as strong or as safe as steel.

d That's crazy! We sell most of our units to France and Germany.

e Yes, but how many people think candles are carrots?

f That's a good idea. We could put all the old files there.

g Yes, you're right. We could operate it from 11.00 p.m. to 7.00 a.m.

h Yes, but that means retraining a lot of our machine operators.

6 Read these dialogues and circle T (true) or F (false).

A **What we need are** flat-panel computer screens.

B **They're too expensive**.

C **I think it's a great idea**. They'll give us much more space on our desks.

B **Yes, but** the screens we have now are only three years old.

A **Why don't we** sell them then?

B **Perhaps, but** who would want our old screens?

C **Exactly!**

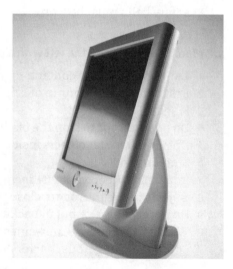

1 A and C think flat-panel screens are a great idea.   (T)/ F

2 B thinks the old screens are good enough.   T / F

3 They all agree the best thing to do is to sell the old screens.   T / F

D **I think we should** install an air-conditioning unit in this room.
E **That's a good idea**. It gets too hot in here in the summer.
F **Maybe, but** then everyone on this side of the building would want one, so we'd have to find somewhere to put a large air-conditioning unit and install pipes. Think of the cost!
D **Yes, you're right**. Perhaps it's not such a good idea.
F **Couldn't we** get some fans?
D **Yes, that's not a bad idea**.
E And **how about** putting up some blinds? They would keep the sun out.
F **Yes, why not?**

4 They agree that installing an air-conditioning unit would be too expensive.   T / F
5 D thinks the idea of installing fans is a good one.   T / F
6 F doesn't think they should put up any blinds.   T / F

G We'll need more space for all these files soon.
H How about scanning them into a PC and putting everything on CD?
J **That's crazy**. It would take ages.
G Why don't we throw some of the old files out?
H Yes, but don't forget there could be some important documents in them.
J Couldn't we hire a couple of students to sort the important stuff out?
G Yes, but how would they know what is important?
J Hmm.

7 They need more room for the files.   T / F
8 J thinks it would be a good idea to put everything on CD.   T / F
9 G agrees that hiring some students to sort the documents out is a good idea.   T / F
10 They can't agree on the best solution.   T / F

7 Read the dialogues in **6** again and write the phrases in bold in the table.

Making a suggestion	Agreeing	Disagreeing
What we need are		

Unit 13

1 Label the pictures with the prepositions in the list.

around   between   ~~along~~   over   through   under   past

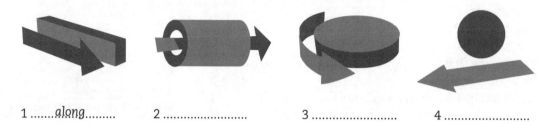

1 ....*along*.........   2 ....   3 ....   4 ....

5 ....   6 ....   7 ....

2 Use the prepositions in the list in **1** to complete these sentences. Use each preposition once.

1 The M25 is a ring road. It goes ......*around*...... London.

2 After you drive .... the pedestrian bridge, you should see our offices on the right.

3 Drive .... this road until you come to a roundabout.

4 Drive .... the supermarket and take the next road on the left.

5 Drive .... the tunnel and take the next exit signposted Taunton.

6 Stay on this road. It goes .... a bridge which crosses the River Dart.

7 The next petrol station is .... Hamstone and Bevington.

3 Look at the map and read the statements. Circle T (true) or F (false). Start at the airport <u>every time</u>. (The airport is in the top left-hand corner of the picture.)

1 Drive out of the airport and turn right. Drive through Dustwood and take the first road on the left. When the road forks, take the left-hand fork. The road takes you to Smallfield. (T)/ F

2 At the end of the road, turn left and get on to the motorway. Drive east along the motorway to junction 10. Turn right and drive south. The first town you come to is Greenhurst. T / F

3 The shortest way to get to Greenhurst from the airport is to drive on to the M90. Take exit 9 to Downing, then turn right at the crossroads. Go over the roundabout in Burstow and turn left at the end of the road. Drive along the A55 to Penstead and take the first exit at the roundabout. Drive through Cockham and the next town is Greenhurst. T / F

4 To get to Penstead from the airport, follow the signs to the motorway. Drive east along the motorway to junction 8 and join the A55 signposted Smallfield and Banfield. Drive through Smallfield and Banfield. The next town you come to is Penstead. T / F

5 It's not the easiest way to get to Godstone Heath, but it is the prettiest. Follow the signs to the motorway and drive east. Leave the motorway at junction 10 and drive south along the road to Edencourt. Take the first road on the right to Warlingstone. Turn left at the T-junction in Warlingstone. The road goes under a railway line and then round the end of Lake Down. When you come to the next T-junction, turn left and drive down the A59. Take the third exit when you come to the roundabout. The next town you come to is Godstone Heath. T / F

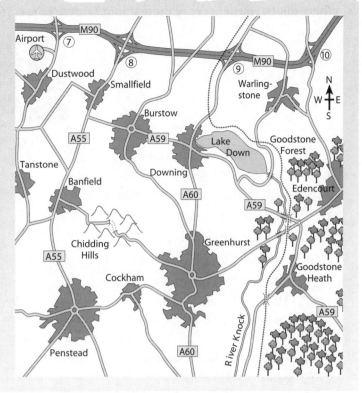

4 Look at the map in 3 again. Complete the dialogue.

A Hello, George. It's Tim here. How many more samples do I have to collect?

B Hello, Tim. Only three. I'll give you the *directions* ¹ . Where are you now?

A I'm driving south ....² the A55 towards Banfield.

B OK, ...³ left when you get to Banfield. The road goes ....⁴ two big hills and then ....⁵ a tunnel. Follow the road until you ....⁶ to the roundabout in Greenhurst. Drive over the ....⁷ .

A Over the ....⁸ ?

B Yes, ...⁹ the second exit. Dr Newby's surgery is on the right-hand ....¹⁰ of the road as you're leaving Greenhurst.

A What's the address?

B 65 Forest Road. Have you got that?

A Yes, I think so.

B Good, then continue driving ....¹¹ that road to Edencourt. The road goes over a ....¹² and under a ....¹³ . Go over the roundabout and drive through the forest to Edencourt. Turn ....¹⁴ in Edencourt and ....¹⁵ the signs to Warlingstone.

A Hang on a second, George. Turn left in Edencourt and ...

B Follow the signs to Warlingstone. Have you got that?

A Listen George, I'll call you again when I've ...

B ... but it's easy. You just have to ...

A George, the signal's breaking up. I'll call you later. Bye.

5 Where might you hear or say these things? Tick (✓) the correct box.

	at an airport	at a car hire company	in a restaurant
1 Can I have the bill, please?	☐	☐	☑
2 The price includes unlimited mileage.	☐	☐	☐
3 Did you pack these bags yourself?	☐	☐	☐
4 Does the price include service?	☐	☐	☐
5 CDW costs another $7.50 per day.	☐	☐	☐
6 I'll need it for three days. So what's the price including insurance?	☐	☐	☐
7 Have you had them with you the whole time?	☐	☐	☐
8 Are you carrying any knives or dangerous instruments?	☐	☐	☐
9 There's a mistake here. I didn't have any wine – just mineral water.	☐	☐	☐
10 Has anyone given you anything to carry?	☐	☐	☐
11 The rest is for you. Thank you.	☐	☐	☐
12 I need to see your driving licence and take your credit card details.	☐	☐	☐
13 Could you open this bag, please, sir?	☐	☐	☐
14 Do you have one that isn't an automatic?	☐	☐	☐
15 Oh, and can you bring me a receipt?	☐	☐	☐

6 Complete the conversation with the words and phrases in the list.

> order   how would you like   bring   Here you are   Can I pay   make it   ~~menu~~
> receipt   list   bill   a mistake   I'd like some

GUEST   Could I have the ......*menu*......¹ and the wine .... ?²

WAITER   Yes, of course ... .,³ sir.

GUEST   Thank you.

          (A *few minutes later*)

WAITER   Are you ready to ....⁴ now, sir?

GUEST   Yes. ....⁵ tomato soup and a steak. Oh, and a glass of Spätburgunder, please.

WAITER   And ....⁶ your steak cooked?

GUEST   Rare, please.

——-

GUEST	Could I have the ....,[7] please?
WAITER	Yes, of course. *(A few minutes later)* Here you are, sir.
GUEST	Thank you. ....[8] by MasterCard?
WAITER	Yes, of course.
GUEST	OK, ...[9] £25 and I need a ....[10]
WAITER	Thank you very much. I'll bring it right away.
GUEST	Oh, just a minute.
WAITER	Yes, sir ...
GUEST	I think there's ....[11] here.
WAITER	Oh dear. What is it?
GUEST	I didn't have any coffee. I only had this glass of wine.
WAITER	I'm sorry, I'll ....[12] you a new bill straightaway.
GUEST	Thank you.

7 **Put the words in the right order to make some questions and sentences a security guard at an airport might say.**

1 yourself / pack / these bags / did you

Did you pack these bags yourself ?

2 has anyone / anything / given you / to carry

.... ?

3 this bag / with you / have you had / the whole time

.... ?

4 or sharp instruments / are you / any knives / carrying

.... ?

5 with you / any electrical items / do you / have

.... ?

6 and passport / see / your boarding card / can I

.... ?

7 put / in this tray / in your pockets / all the metal objects

....

8 all the electrical items / open / and take out / that bag / in it

....

8 **The passenger in 7 didn't have any problems with airport security. Match his / her replies in the list to questions 1–6.**

No, I'm not.   Of course. Here you are.   No, they haven't.   ~~Yes, I did.~~   Yes, I have.   No, I don't.

Question 1 *Yes, I did.*   Question 4 ....

Question 2 ....   Question 5 ....

Question 3 ....   Question 6 ....

Unit 14

1 Read the information about the largest ocean liner in the world, Queen Mary 2, and complete the text with the figures in the list.

55 km/h	150,000 tonnes	16 km	72 m	345 m	5
2004	18 m²	1,250	6 days	137 m²	~~$800,000,000~~

Queen Mary 2 is the largest and most luxurious passenger ship ever built. It cost an estimated $800,000,000 ....¹ to build and equip her*. The facilities include ten restaurants, ...² swimming pools, a spa, a casino, a theatre, and a planetarium.

With a top speed of .... ,³ the QM2 can cross the Atlantic in less than ....⁴ She made her maiden voyage across the Atlantic in .... .⁵

At .... ,⁶ she is over 30 m longer than the Eiffel Tower is high. She is ....⁷ tall, that's as tall as a 21-storey building, and she is 45 metres wide. She weighs about .... .⁸

She can accommodate over 2,620 passengers and ....⁹ crew members. The standard cabins are only .... ,¹⁰ but if you have a lot of money and want to cruise in real luxury, the Queen Mary suite offers you a bit more space, ... ,¹¹ and comes with a butler.

Finally, one more amazing statistic, the ship's whistle can be heard up to ....¹² away.

*We normally say 'it' for things, but we can use 'she' to talk about ships.

2 Which figures in the list in **1** refer to dimensions (the size – length, width, height, etc. – of something)?

Dimensions:

16 km

....

....

3 Which figures in the list in **1** refer to:

1 speed? ..55 km/h..............

2 price? ....

3 date? ....

4 number? ....

5 weight? ....

6 length of time? ....

4 Complete the list.

Noun	Adjective
1 height	high
2	long
3 width	....
4	heavy
5 age	....
6	deep
7 speed	....

5 Use the appropriate adjective from the table in **4** to make questions.

1 How ..high.............. is Mount Kilimanjaro?
It's 5,893 metres high.

2 How .... is Stonehenge?
It was built about 5,000 years ago.

3 How .... is the Airbus 380?
Well, the wingspan is 80 metres.

4 How .... does light travel?
The speed of light is about 300,000,000 metres per second.

5 How .... is the Pacific Ocean?
Well, the Marianas Trench in the Pacific Ocean is 11,033 metres below sea level.

6 How .... is the River Thames?
It's 338 km from the source in the Cotswold Hills to its mouth in the North Sea.

7 How .... is the Eiffel Tower?
The total weight is 8.56 million kg, or 8,560 tonnes.

6 Complete the sentences with *tall* or *high*.

1 I'm 158 cm ..tall......... .

2 How .... is the ceiling?

3 The Empire State Building is 448 metres ....

4 How .... can you reach?

5 The crates are 1.5 m long, 1 m wide, and 1.25 m ....

6 Do you know how .... these trees can grow?

7 How .... can passenger planes fly?

8 Robert Wadlow was 2.72 metres ....

7 Complete the text with *is / are* or *isn't / aren't*.

Pete and I work from home. Pete runs a company that installs satellite dishes and I do everything else – if there ......*are*.......[1] bills that have to be sent out, I write them. If there ....[2] a problem, I try to sort it out, or send Pete round to fix it. There ....[3] much room in my office and there ....[4] enough space on the desk for a telephone. I'd like to have a few plants in the office, but there ....[5] a window, so there ....[6] any plants.

Pete doesn't help the situation – there ....[7] three of his surfboards and a pair of water-skis in the office, too! There ....[8] days when I wish I had a proper office, but there ....[9] much point complaining about it. We're slowly building up the business. One day we'll have a bigger house – with a proper office in it!

8 Complete the sentences with *much, many, a little,* or *a few*.

1 How ....*much*........ time do we have to complete the project?

2 I need to make .... copies before we start.

3 How .... copies do you need?

4 There aren't .... of these units left. I think we should order some more.

5 How .... data is stored on this server?

6 I think we'll all need to have .... break after such a hard week.

7 There isn't .... pressure in these tyres. They need pumping up.

8 There are still .... bugs in this program, but we should be able to fix them all by the end of next week.

9 This new process produces .... CO_2, but not much.

10 How .... workers were injured at the plant last year?

9 Match the questions and statements on the left with the replies on the right.

1 We have three months to deliver this order.
2 I get about three emails a month.
3 We normally use ten toner cartridges a month, so I've ordered 20. Is that OK?
4 He wants £25,000 for his rusty, old motorbike.
5 I've changed the oil in the car and I poured a litre of oil into the engine.
6 Are there a lot of staff here in August?
7 Is there enough space in the cellar to store these old PCs?
8 Do you have a lot of money with you?

a That's not enough.
b No, only a little.
c That's not many.
d That's plenty of time.
e Yes, there's plenty.
f That's too much.
g No, only a few.
h Yes, that's enough.

Unit 15

1 Complete the dialogue with the words and phrases in the list.

> take   need   tied up   by   to confirm   free   check
> ~~make it~~   schedule   a note   How about   say

PETER   Peter Cookson.

GEORGE   Oh, hello, Peter. It's George here. I'm ringing about the meeting next week. I'm afraid I can't ..._make it_...[1] on Wednesday. I have to visit one of our suppliers. Are you ....[2] on Tuesday or Thursday?

PETER   Let me have a look at my ....[3] I'm ....[4] on Tuesday, but I'm free on Thursday afternoon.

GEORGE   Thursday afternoon, OK. Well, I have a meeting with the quality circle at one o'clock, but it shouldn't ....[5] more than an hour. ....[6] two-thirty?

PETER   OK, let's ....[7] two-thirty, then. I'll have to ....[8] that with Laura to see if she's free then. I'll call you back later ....[9]

GEORGE   OK, I'll make ....[10] of that, Thursday, two-thirty. How long do you think we'll ....?[11]

PETER   An hour should be long enough.

GEORGE   So we should finish ....[12] three-thirty.

2 Complete the dialogue with _by_ or _until_.

SARAH   We need to arrange a meeting about the shut-down in July. How about Monday morning?

JAMES   Yes, Monday's OK for me, but Jan won't have the production plan data we need ...._by_....[1] Monday. We'll have to wait ....[2] they've had the planning meeting on Wednesday morning.

SARAH   Well, I'll be out of the office ....[3] about 12.30 on Wednesday. How about 1.30?

JAMES   Jan won't have everything ready ....[4] then. Can't we wait ....[5] Thursday?

SARAH   Thursday? Let me think ... I'm visiting a new supplier on Thursday morning, but I should be back ....[6] 2.00. How long do you think the meeting will take?

JAMES   At least two hours. We should finish ....[7] 4.30. Why?

SARAH   I'm flying to Paris on Thursday evening. I have to be at the airport ....[8] 6.00.

JAMES   Well, you could stay ....[9] 4.00. We should have covered most of the points ....[10] then and I can fill you in later. By the way, when do you get back?

SARAH   I'll be in Paris ....[11] Monday. I'll be back on Tuesday.

3 **Match a phrase on the left with an equivalent phrase on the right.**

1 I'm tied up next week.
2 How about next week, then?
3 We need to finish by ten-thirty.
4 I can't make it at ten-thirty.
5 I can manage ten-thirty.
6 I'll call you back to confirm.
7 I'm very short of time.
8 How long will that take?

a Ten-thirty's OK.
b We'll have to finish before ten-thirty.
c I'll phone you later to let you know.
d I have a really busy schedule.
e I'm busy next week.
f I'm afraid ten-thirty isn't possible.
g Let's say next week, then.
h How long do you think we'll need?

4 **Complete the table using the phrases in the list.**

I can't make ten, but I can manage eleven.

Half an hour should be long enough.

Are you free on Friday?

I'll talk to Sue and confirm it later.

I'm afraid I'm busy then.

I won't be back until 2.30.

Wednesday at 10 is fine.

I can't make 8.30, I'm afraid.

That's good for me.

Shall we say six-thirty?

I'm tied up most of this week, but next week's better.

OK, I'll meet you there at nine o'clock.

How about 12.30?

OK, let's say three-thirty in your office, then.

How long do we need?

Yes, I'm free then.

No, I'm afraid I can't manage Tuesday.

How long do you think it'll take?

Suggesting a time	Saying 'Yes'
Saying when you are available	**Saying 'No'**
I can't make ten, but I can manage eleven.	
Estimating time	**Confirming arrangements**

5 **Look at Dave Bradley's diary and read the sentences below. Circle T (true) or F (false).**

1 Dave's tied up on Monday morning.   (T)/ F
2 The quality circle meeting will last about 90 minutes.   T / F
3 He has to pick up the car by 4.30.   T / F
4 Dave has two meetings on Tuesday.   T / F
5 He couldn't arrange a two-hour meeting on Wednesday.   T / F
6 He won't be at the office until about 2.00 on Thursday.   T / F
7 He'll be in a meeting at 10.00 on Friday, but he's free from 4.30.   T / F
8 Dave's arranged to help a friend install a PC at the weekend.   T / F
9 Dave hasn't made any arrangements to meet anyone on Sunday.   T / F

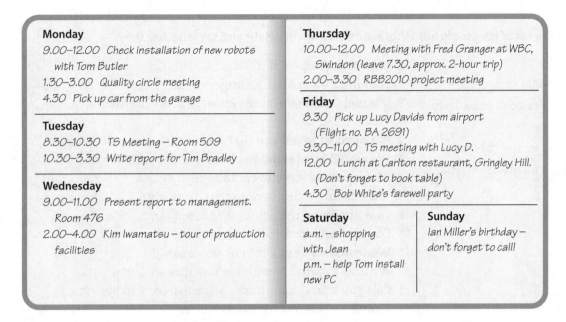

Monday
9.00–12.00 Check installation of new robots with Tom Butler
1.30–3.00 Quality circle meeting
4.30 Pick up car from the garage

Tuesday
8.30–10.30 TS Meeting – Room 509
10.30–3.30 Write report for Tim Bradley

Wednesday
9.00–11.00 Present report to management. Room 476
2.00–4.00 Kim Iwamatsu – tour of production facilities

Thursday
10.00–12.00 Meeting with Fred Granger at WBC, Swindon (leave 7.30, approx. 2-hour trip)
2.00–3.30 RBB2010 project meeting

Friday
8.30 Pick up Lucy Davids from airport (Flight no. BA 2691)
9.30–11.00 TS meeting with Lucy D.
12.00 Lunch at Carlton restaurant, Gringley Hill. (Don't forget to book table)
4.30 Bob White's farewell party

Saturday
a.m. – shopping with Jean
p.m. – help Tom install new PC

Sunday
Ian Miller's birthday – don't forget to call!

6 Complete these emails using the phrases in the list.

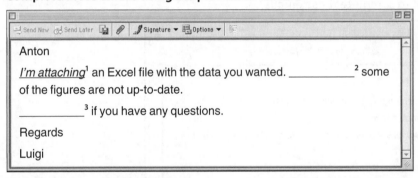

Anton

I'm attaching[1] an Excel file with the data you wanted. _____[2] some of the figures are not up-to-date.

_____[3] if you have any questions.

Regards

Luigi

Dear Mr Franklin,

_____[4] the problems you had with our last shipment of electric motors. We are sending you another shipment today. _____[5] return the units you have? We will credit your account with the transportation costs.

_____[6]

David Wilkinson

Please could you
Looking forward to
Do you want me to
Please get back to me
Yours sincerely
~~I'm attaching~~
Please confirm
Thank you for
We are sorry about
We would be happy to
I'm afraid that
Sorry

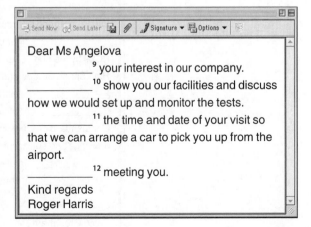

Hello Carlos

_____[7] I haven't got back to you sooner, but I was in Singapore last week.

You said in your email that you have a problem opening the last file I sent you. I think it could be a problem with the version you're using. We've just upgraded to the latest version (v10.5).

_____[8] convert it to v9.0 and resend it?

Barry

Dear Ms Angelova

_____[9] your interest in our company.

_____[10] show you our facilities and discuss how we would set up and monitor the tests.

_____[11] the time and date of your visit so that we can arrange a car to pick you up from the airport.

_____[12] meeting you.

Kind regards
Roger Harris

7 Look at the list of phrases in bold that are often used in emails and say whether they:

a offer help
b ask people to do things
c introduce good or bad news
d thank people
e refer to future contact
f refer to an attachment.

1 **I'm sorry, (but)** we can't ....c....
2 **Looking forward to** meeting you. ....
3 **(Please) Could you** let me know as soon as possible? ....
4 **Thx** a lot. ....
5 **I'm pleased to tell you** that we can give you a 3% discount. ....
6 **We would be pleased to** produce these parts for you. ....
7 **I'd appreciate it if you could** send ... .
8 **Thanks for** getting back to me so quickly. ....
9 **I am attaching** the figures you asked for. ....
10 **I'm afraid (that)** we don't have any ... .
11 **We would be happy to** send you a sample. ....
12 **We look forward to** working together with you. ....
13 **Can you** sign the contract and send it back to me? ....
14 **Thank you for** letting us know about ... .

8 Use some of the phrases in **7** to complete these emails.

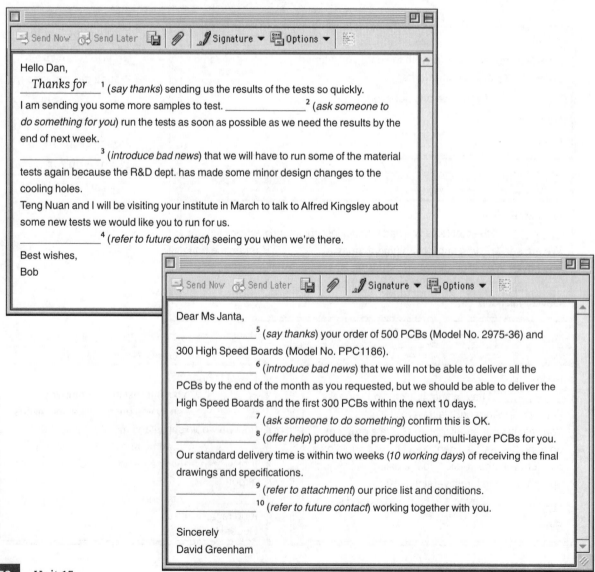

Send Now   Send Later   Signature ▼   Options ▼

Hello Dan,

_____Thanks for_____ ¹ (*say thanks*) sending us the results of the tests so quickly.
I am sending you some more samples to test. _____² (*ask someone to do something for you*) run the tests as soon as possible as we need the results by the end of next week.
_____³ (*introduce bad news*) that we will have to run some of the material tests again because the R&D dept. has made some minor design changes to the cooling holes.
Teng Nuan and I will be visiting your institute in March to talk to Alfred Kingsley about some new tests we would like you to run for us.
_____⁴ (*refer to future contact*) seeing you when we're there.

Best wishes,
Bob

Send Now   Send Later   Signature ▼   Options ▼

Dear Ms Janta,

_____⁵ (*say thanks*) your order of 500 PCBs (Model No. 2975-36) and 300 High Speed Boards (Model No. PPC1186).
_____⁶ (*introduce bad news*) that we will not be able to deliver all the PCBs by the end of the month as you requested, but we should be able to deliver the High Speed Boards and the first 300 PCBs within the next 10 days.
_____⁷ (*ask someone to do something*) confirm this is OK.
_____⁸ (*offer help*) produce the pre-production, multi-layer PCBs for you. Our standard delivery time is within two weeks (*10 working days*) of receiving the final drawings and specifications.
_____⁹ (*refer to attachment*) our price list and conditions.
_____¹⁰ (*refer to future contact*) working together with you.

Sincerely
David Greenham

Unit 16

1 Underline the person who would say these things.

1 I'm happy with the quality, but what kind of discount can you offer us if we buy 10,000?
   a supplier   b logistics manager   c <u>purchaser</u>

2 There's always a big demand for our products in December, so we have to outsource some of the work to shipping companies.
   a purchaser   b logistics manager   c production manager

3 We give feedback on which products are selling best to our headquarters in London.
   a store manager   b logistics manager   c purchaser

4 We can't manufacture 5,000 units by the end of the month without a second shift.
   a logistics manager   b production manager   c purchaser

5 OK, so we've agreed on the price, now what about delivery times?
   a purchaser   b logistics manager   c production manager

2 Match a word on the left with a word on the right to make a fixed expression.

1 competitive	a chain
2 finished	b companies
3 just-in-time	c cycle times
4 lead	d market
5 product	e outlets
6 retail	f products
7 shipping	g production
8 supply	h times

3 Complete the sentences using the expressions in **2**.

1 We transport some of the goods ourselves, but we outsource most of this work to ......*shipping*...... *companies* .

2 We have to make sure we use the latest technology and keep our prices as low as possible. We operate in a very ....

3 Thanks to a more flexible manufacturing process, we have managed to reduce our .... from three weeks to ten days.

4 Our suppliers deliver the parts when we need them. We can't afford to keep large stocks of parts. .... helps keep our costs down.

5 The .... are stored in our warehouse until they are shipped to the customer.

6 At one end of the .... are the suppliers of the raw materials. At the other end of it are the customers.

7 Wal-Mart has over 4,800 .... worldwide.

8 .... in the car industry have fallen by about 50% in the last few years. New models are produced every two to three years.

4 The pictures show the seven steps that are used to recycle plastic in the correct order. Label the pictures with the words in the box.

> washing   filtering   inspection   pelletizing and re-manufacture   melting
> ~~flotation tank~~   drying

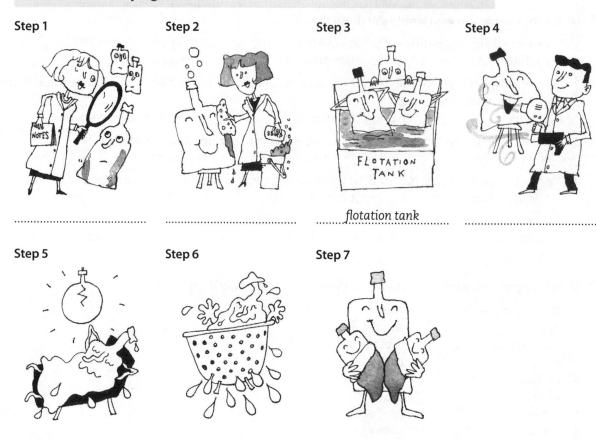

Step 1 ....

Step 2 ....

Step 3 *flotation tank*

Step 4 ....

Step 5 ....

Step 6 ....

Step 7 ....

5 Now read about the process of recycling plastic and use the pictures in **4** to number the steps.

.... **a** After that the plastic is dried in a tumble drier.

.... **b** The molten plastic is forced through a fine filter to remove any unwanted materials that slipped through the washing process. The molten plastic is then formed into thin strands like spaghetti.

.... **c** The strands are cooled in water and chopped into small pieces called pellets. Manufacturing companies buy the plastic pellets from recyclers to make new products. Recycled plastics can be made into things such as flowerpots and carpets.

...1... **d** Workers inspect the plastic waste for contaminants like rock and glass, and for plastics that the plant cannot recycle.

.... **e** Next, it is put into a machine called an extruder which heats the plastic under pressure. Different types of plastic melt at different temperatures.

.... **f** Then the plastic is washed and shredded.

.... **g** If mixed plastics are being recycled, they are sorted in a flotation tank. Some types of plastic sink and others float.

6 Complete the dialogues using the words in the list.

| throw away | take apart | sort out | ~~take out~~ | blow up | heat up | cut up |

1 A It's going to be a big job to rewire all these offices.

  B Yes, but we don't have to replace the electricity cables. We only have to .....*take out*..... the old computer cables and put the new ones in.

2 A Why isn't there a warning sign on this tank?

  B A warning sign? Why do we need to put up a warning sign?

  A Because it's full of liquid hydrogen. If the tank leaks and someone smokes in here, it could ....

3 A I can't get all these cardboard boxes into this recycling bin.

  B Of course you can, but you need to .... them .... first.

4 A The gearbox is still making a funny noise.

  B Is it? Well, we'll just have to .... it .... and see if we can find what's causing it.

5 A How do you .... all the different types of plastics?

  B We use a special machine called an infrared spectroscope to identify them.

6 A And how do you get rid of the stress?

  B We slowly .... the parts .... to 350 °C and then let them cool. That gets rid of most of the stress.

7 A What are you going to do with all those bottles?

  B I'm going to .... them .... Why?

  A You can't do that. You should take them to a bottle bank so that the glass can be recycled.

7 Use the two-part verbs in **6** to replace the words in bold.

1 We use this machine to **shred** the recycled plastic.
We use this machine to .....*cut*..... the recycled plastic .....*up*....... .

2 First, you need to take the cover off and **remove** the film.
First, you need to take the cover off and .... the film ....

3 Are you sure it's a good idea to **dismantle** it? You might not be able to put it back together again.
Are you sure it's a good idea to .... it .... ? You might not be able to put it back together again.

4 Can you **discard** old televisions as household waste?
Can you .... old televisions .... as household waste?

5 We can't store those drums in here. They're full of ammonia and could **explode**.
We can't store those drums in here. They're full of ammonia and could ....

6 We need to **identify** which materials we can recycle and which we can dispose of.
We need to .... which materials we can recycle and which we can dispose of.

7 The engine doesn't work very efficiently when it's cold. It needs to **get hotter** first.
The engine doesn't work very efficiently when it's cold. It needs to .... first.

8 Complete the crossword.

Across

2 We can recycle 90% of the materials. The 10% that's _____ is burnt. (4)

4 The next step is to _____ and shred the plastic. (4)

6 Batteries are difficult to recycle, but it's _____ to recycle paper. (4)

8 We began using recycled paper about ten years _____ (3)

9 We don't _____ the tyres in the ground. We sell them to the cement industry. (4)

11 The red _____ should be connected to the positive side of the battery and the black _____ to the negative side. (4)

13 We store the finished _____ in that warehouse over there. (8)

15 Our suppliers deliver the parts we need when we need them. This is called _____ production. (4,2,4)

19 Another word for *cut up*. (5)

20 The verb of *competition*. (7)

21 *Water, oil, petrol,* and *brake fluid* are _____. (7)

23 We _____ the plastic here. PVC goes into that bin, PETE goes into this bin, and PP goes over there. (4)

24 Cut those cardboard boxes up and _____ them into that bin over there. (3)

25 A supply _____ starts with the producers of the raw materials and ends with the customer. (5)

26 To press something together very hard. (5)

27 Product _____ times in the car industry are getting shorter and shorter. (5)

Down

1 One of the first things we do when we recycle a car is to drain the petrol from the _____. (4)

2 We can save money by keeping our inventories _____. (3)

3 We have to _____ all the liquids from the car. (5)

5 We _____ the finished goods in the warehouse. (5)

7 Another word for *changed* or *modified*. (7)

10 We _____ about 10% of the production. We produce 90% of the parts we need in-house. (9)

12 Parts that are still almost new aren't recycled. They can be _____. (6)

14 Another word for *explode*. (4,2)

16 New movements and / or directions. (6)

17 Don't _____ those batteries away! They can be recharged. (5)

18 You can _____ plastic if you heat it up. (4)

22 We _____ the goods from this central warehouse to our stores. (4)

Unit 17

1 Label the picture using the words in the list.

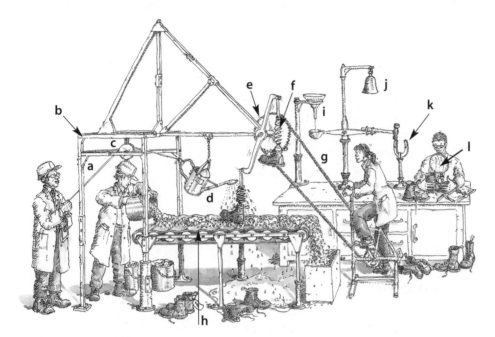

1 bell
2 chain
3 pulley
4 frame
5 magnet
6 string
7 belt
8 spring
9 cog
10 magnifying glass
11 watering can
12 funnel

2 Read the description of the equipment and how the shoes are tested. Complete the text using the words and phrases in the list.

are hinged	fall	inspect	is held in place	are attached to	is supported by	clockwise
~~test~~	pulls	move	turns	drops	wear	rises	is connected to	downwards

This is where we _____test_____¹ the shoes. The woman sitting on the thing that looks like a bicycle without wheels _____² the pedals. The chain _____³ a large cog over the belt. The cog is bolted to the frame. The two legs on the cog _____⁴ so that they can bend. There's a spring at the end of the legs. The springs _____⁵ wooden feet inside the shoes. The springs put pressure on the shoes when they hit the belt and turn the belt _____.⁶ A man at the end of the belt _____⁷ sand, small stones, and other objects on to the belt to simulate real walking conditions. These objects _____⁸ along the belt and _____⁹ into a box at the end. We also test the shoes to see if they are waterproof. We use a watering can to simulate rain. When the man _____¹⁰ the string, it tips the watering can and sprinkles water on to the shoes.

We time all the tests. We use a funnel full of sand. The funnel _____¹¹ a stand. The sand slowly trickles out of the bottom of the funnel into a cup at one end of a balance. At the other end of the balance, there's a hammer head which _____¹² by a magnet. When there's enough sand in the cup, the magnet is not strong enough to hold the hammer head and the balance tips on the pivot. The cup moves _____¹³ and the hammer _____¹⁴ and hits the bell.

After the test we _____¹⁵ all the shoes for _____¹⁶ and tear, and check to see if any water has soaked into the shoes.

3 Look at the picture in **1** and circle T (true) or F (false).

1 The funnel is supported by a stand. (T)/ F
2 The shoes are bolted to the belt. T / F
3 The legs are hinged. T / F
4 The watering can is suspended from a hook. T / F
5 The belt is supported by eight legs. T / F
6 The two cogs are clamped to the frames. T / F
7 The string is attached to a pulley. T / F
8 The boots are secured to springs. T / F
9 The two cogs are linked by a chain. T / F
10 The hammer head and cup are pivoted. T / F

4 Underline the correct phrase.

1 These two buildings .... a bridge.
  a are screwed to   b <u>are linked by</u>   c are suspended by

2 The printer .... the back of the PC with a USB cable.
  a is clamped to   b is hinged to   c is connected to

3 The wheels .... the truck's axles.
  a are bolted to   b are screwed to   c are tied to

4 The ship's anchor .... a chain.
  a is housed in   b is attached to   c is pivoted by

5 Those balloons need to .... some string.
  a be tied to   b be hinged to   c be secured to

6 One side of a door has to .... the door frame.
  a be clamped to   b be bolted to   c be hinged to

7 The film and the batteries .... the camera.
  a are tied to   b are housed in   c are hooked to

8 This building .... steel beams.
  a is clamped to   b is chained to   c is supported by

5 Read the dialogue and label the diagram.

TOM   Hello, Olaf. What are you doing?

OLAF   Oh, hello, Tom. I'm trying to repair my bike. It's making a funny noise. I think it's the pedals.

TOM   Let's have a look .... No, it's not the pedals. It feels like the bearings in the bottom bracket are worn. They need replacing.

OLAF   The bottom bracket. What's that?

TOM   It's the bit that connects the two cranks.

OLAF   Oh ... and is it a big job to repair?

TOM   Well, it's not too difficult if you have the right tools. You can borrow mine.

OLAF   Oh thanks, but what do I have to do?

TOM   Well, the first thing you have to do is to remove the cranks. You have to take off the dust cap on each crank and unscrew the bolts that fit into the end of the spindle. Oh yes, and there's a washer between the bolts and the crank, so remove the washers too.

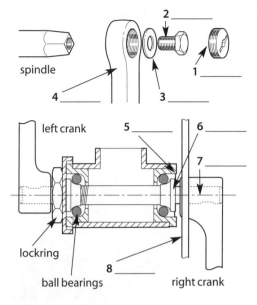

spindle

left crank

lockring

ball bearings

right crank

OLAF Which crank should I take off first?

TOM It doesn't really matter. I'd take off the right crank with the chain ring first.

OLAF OK.

TOM The bit that sticks out on either side of the frame is the spindle. You have to remove that to get at the ball bearings. They're housed between a cup that's screwed into the frame and a cone on the spindle. You have to unscrew the lock ring on the left of the left-hand side of the spindle and remove the cone.

OLAF That doesn't sound too difficult.

TOM No, just replace the ball bearings and you need to lubricate the ball bearings, so don't forget to put some grease into the area between the cups and the cones. If you need any help, just let me know.

OLAF Thanks, Tom.

6 Look at the diagram of an electric water pump and circle T (true) or F (false).

1 wet end cover
2 cover gasket
3 impeller
4 seal assembly
5 wet end housing
6 O-ring
7 inlet tube
8 outlet tube

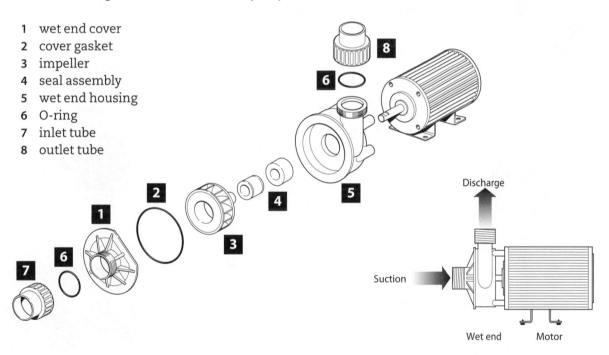

Discharge

Suction

Wet end   Motor

1 The wet end cover is connected to the front of the pump.		(T)/ F
2 The motor through bolt screws into the impeller.		T / F
3 Water flows through the inlet tube and out of the drain plug.		T / F
4 The motor is located in the middle of the pump.		T / F
5 The seal assembly is located behind the impeller and in front of the wet end housing.		T / F
6 The cylindrical tube that sticks out of the motor turns the wet end cover.		T / F
7 A drain plug fits into the wet end cover.		T / F
8 The cover gasket fits between the wet end cover and the drain plug.		T / F
9 The motor is fastened to the wet end.		T / F

7 Look at the pictures and complete the sentences with the words and phrases in the list.

behind   above   on the back of   ~~on top of~~   under   in front of   on the front of
on the bottom of

1   The dish is ....*on top of*.......... the radio telescope.

2   The screens are .... the man.

3   The aero-engines are .... the wings.

4   The steel beam is .... the construction worker.

5   The label is .... the bottle.

6   The warning signs are .... the lorry*.

7   There are four wheels .... this trolley.

8   The turbines are .... the blades.

lorry **BrE** – truck **AmE**

Unit 18

1 Is digital photography better than film photography? Read about the advantages and disadvantages and circle T (true) or F (false).

Digital Photography

Advantages	Disadvantages
● Newer technology with lots of interesting features and gadgets.	● High quality films have a higher resolution.
● You can edit the images easily on a PC.	● Good digital cameras are more expensive.
● Small size of many cameras makes them easier to carry.	● Most digital camera do not have lenses you can change.
● You can look at the images immediately and delete the images you don't want.	● You normally need a computer and special software to work on your images.
● You can make good quality prints on an inexpensive desktop printer.	● The small size of many digital cameras makes them difficult to hold steady.
● You can choose the size and quality of the images.	● Cameras have many features you may never need or understand.
● You can store and manage the images on your PC or copy them to CDs.	● Most digital cameras are fully automatic so the photographer has little control.
● You can easily send the images in emails or put them on a website.	● You need a power supply to charge the batteries.
● You don't need to spend time and money developing a film.	● The technology ages quickly.
	● Only the more expensive cameras have interchangeable lenses.
	● The instruction manual is often heavier than the camera.

1 Film cameras can take better quality pictures.   (T)/ F
2 Digital cameras are normally lighter and smaller than film cameras.   T / F
3 Film cameras are usually more expensive.   T / F
4 It's easier and quicker to print images from a digital camera.   T / F
5 Digital cameras are more reliable if you are not near electrical power.   T / F
6 It's easier to find different lenses for film cameras.   T / F
7 It's more difficult to publish an image from a film camera on a website.   T / F
8 You can see an image of the picture you have taken faster with a film camera.   T / F

2 Complete the sentences using the comparative form of the word in brackets.

1 Film cameras are (cheap) ....*cheaper*.... than digital cameras.

2 Flying by plane is (safe) .... than riding a motorbike.

3 I think this machine would work (well) .... if we replaced the bearings.

4 You can see the structure of the material (clearly) .... in the next slide.

5 It's much (fast) .... to email a message than to send it by post.

6 Can you come a bit (early) .... tomorrow?

7 I'll ask Antonio to explain it to you. His English is (good) .... than mine.

8 This type of drug need to be much (carefully) .... tested in future.

9 Laser jets are (expensive) .... than ink jets, but the print quality is (high) ....

10 Be careful how you lift that box. It's a lot (heavy) .... than the other two.

11 I'm sure we could produce these parts (cheaply) .... than we do now if we used robots.

12 We need to respond to complaints (fast) .... than we have in the past.

3 Complete the conversations using the phrases in the list.

Conversation A

can't afford that   are you sure   ~~What's the problem?~~   Why don't we

A ATP isn't happy about the last shipment of frames we sent them.

B Why? *What's the problem?*[1]

A Most of them were scratched and two were bent.

C And ....[2] they were OK when they left the factory?

A Yes.

B It sounds like the shipping agent again. ....[3] change the company we use?

C But that will be the third time we've changed the shipping agent this year. How about buying a couple of lorries and shipping the frames ourselves?

B We ....[4] Why don't we improve the way the frames are packed?

A OK, I'll see what we can do, but it will mean higher packing and shipping costs.

Conversation B

not ready yet   the hold-up   don't forget   speed them up   are we going to do   nothing else

A We're not going to meet the production schedule for the GP-497 parts.

B What's ....?[5]

A Well, one of the presses broke down last week. Maintenance is working to fix the problem, but it's ....[6]

C Can't you do anything to ....?[7]

A No, the hold-up is with the spare parts. We won't get the spares until next week.

B Can't we outsource the work?

C Yes, but ....[8] all the problems we had last time we outsourced work.

A Yes, we had to scrap 15% of the parts and rework the rest.

B Do we have any spare capacity on the other presses?

A No, I'm afraid not.

C What ....[9] then?

A We'll just have to delay the schedule. There's ....[10] we can do.

Conversation C

> to solve   long enough   go out of   won't that be   It should be   a big risk to take

A We'll only have two weeks to re-equip the workshop this summer.

B Why's that?

A Because the plant manager wants us to do it in the two weeks the plant closes.

C Is that .... ?[11]

A ....[12] if we work around the clock and at the weekends.

B Yes, but ....[13] very expensive?

C Yes, but not as expensive as paying 85 production staff to stay at home and do nothing.

A Yes, and we still have one big problem ....[14]

B What's that?

A Well, the company that is supplying the machining centres is in financial difficulty. They could .... [15] business.

C Can't we switch suppliers?

A Yes, but this company has always been very reliable and it would cost us a lot of money to cancel the order now.

B Hmm, it's .... ,[16] but I don't think we have any alternative.

4 Read the conversations in **3** again. Which conversation is about:

1 time and money? ....   2 quality and money? ....   3 time and quality? ....

5 Look at the sentences and decide whether they are about time (T), quality (Q), or money (M).

1 If we want it to last, we should use steel parts. ....T......

2 What kind of discount can you give us if we pay cash? ....

3 It'll take too long to ship these parts by boat. ....

4 This model is very unreliable. We'll have to replace it soon. ....

5 We can't afford any more hold-ups. ....

6 I think we should outsource these parts if we can't produce them more economically. ....

7 We'll have to buy in the shafts if we want to meet the deadline. ....

8 We can't produce the gears to these specs. The tolerances are too small. ....

6 Complete the sentences using the correct form of the words in brackets.

1 If we (make) ...*make*..... these parts out of plastic, we (save) ...*'ll save*..... a lot of weight.

2 We (not meet) .... the deadline if you can't (fix) .... the problem today.

3 He (install) .... the software for free if we (buy) .... more than twenty licences.

4 If you (need) .... to make any changes, we (send) .... you the plans.

5 We (have) .... to find a new supplier if the quality of their products (not improve)
....

6 I (send) .... a technician to you if you (cannot) .... solve the problem.

7 **Match a phrase on the left with a phrase on the right.**

1 The best way to fix a shelf to a wall
2 The quickest way to send the figures
3 The most reliable way to check the circuit
4 The simplest way to pay for a taxi ride
5 The most environmentally friendly way to transport goods
6 The most economical way to phone from a public telephone box
7 The safest way to store heating oil
8 The easiest way to double your money

a is with a voltmeter.
b is by rail.
c is with brackets and screws.
d is to use a double-walled tank.
e is by email.

f is to fold it once and put it back in your pocket.
g is with cash.
h is with a pre-paid card.

8 **Complete the crossword.**

Across

3 If the machine doesn't _____, call a service engineer. (4)
6 To go round a place or building at regular times to make sure it is safe and that nothing is wrong. (6)
7 When you buy a better or higher version of something, you _____ . (7)
10 No longer useful because something better has been invented. (8)
14 We won't finish the project on _____ . We need two more days. (4)
16 The fire at the supplier's factory could _____ some delivery delays. (5)
17 If we make the part out of steel, it should _____ longer. (4)
18 This is a very difficult problem to _____ . (5)
19 The superlative of *easy*. (7)
20 What's the _____ environmentally friendly way of disposing of old oil? (4)

Down

1 A person who protects a place or people. (5)
2 A building where large quantities of goods are stored. (9)
3 The adverb of *good*. (4)
4 I speak French badly, but my Italian is _____ . (5)
5 A sum of money that can be spent for a specific purpose in a certain period of time. (6)
8 The biggest _____ is that we don't have enough money to buy new computers. (7)
9 Detailed information about how something should be made or built. (5)
11 This phone was _____ designed. Some of the buttons are in the wrong place. (5)
12 This program is expensive, but that one is even _____ expensive. (4)
13 The superlative of *good*. (4)
15 _____ we cut some corners, we'll save a lot of time. (2)

Unit 19

1 **Read the story about Charles Babbage and put the verbs in brackets into the past passive.**

Charles Babbage was born in London on December 26, 1791. He taught himself algebra and mathematics and went to Trinity College in Cambridge.

After leaving university, Babbage (employ) _was employed_ [1] as a mathematician. He (ask) ....[2] to join the Royal Society in 1816 and helped to set up the Royal Astronomical Society. It was about this time that he became interested in the idea of developing a calculating machine.

Babbage began constructing a small calculating machine in 1819 and the machine (build) ....[3] in 1822.

Babbage (give) ....[4] £1,500 by the British government to develop a much larger calculator with a printer that could print out the sums. The money soon ran out. A lot more money (need) .... [5] Babbage (give) ....[6] a total of £17,000 by the government and he invested another £6,000 of his own money into the project.

Government funding (stop) ....[7] in 1834, but Babbage had other plans. He wanted to develop an analytical engine. It (design) ....[8] to run on steam and it had a 'memory' that could hold 1000 numbers of 50 digits each, but Babbage designed the analytic engine to have infinite storage. This (do) ....[9] by outputting data to punched cards which could be read into the machine again later.

Although the mechanical computer (not build) ....[10] in Babbage's lifetime, the design has been proved correct and recently such a computer (construct) ....[11] following Babbage's own design criteria – and it worked!

2 **Read the text in 1 again and circle T (true) or F (false).**

1 Babbage was born at the end of the eighteenth century. (T)/ F
2 He was taught algebra and mathematics before he went to university. T / F
3 He was invited to join the Royal Astronomical Society. T / F
4 The first machine that was built was a small calculating machine. T / F
5 The British government was asked to build a larger calculating machine with a printer. T / F
6 The government stopped funding the project in 1834. T / F
7 The analytical engine was powered by steam. T / F
8 A computer was used to build the analytical engine using Babbage's design criteria. T / F

3 Read about these inventions and complete the questions.

The first electronic computer, the ENIAC, was built by the US army in 1945. It weighed over 30 tonnes and consumed 200 kilowatts.

1 Who was ..._the first electronic computer built by_...?

2 When was ....?

The first personal computer was produced by IBM in 1975. It was called the IBM 5100. It was equipped with 64K of memory and cost $19,975.

3 Who was ....?

4 How much memory was ....?

The first pocket calculator was called the Curta. It was invented by Curt Herzstark and produced in Liechtenstein. The first calculators went on sale in 1948.

5 Who was ....?

6 Where was ....?

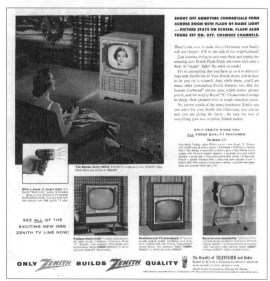

The first wireless remote control unit for a televison was called 'Flashmatic'. It was produced by Zenith Radio Corporation in 1955.

7 What was ....?

8 When was ....?

4 Complete the dialogue using the verbs in the list.

| called | installed | ~~Has~~ | had | didn't have | 've checked | came | haven't | have | did | fix | told |

MARTIN ....*Has*..........¹ all the equipment arrived yet?

HARALD Oh, hello, Martin. Yes, it ....² yesterday afternoon.

MARTIN Oh, good. Have you installed everything?

HARALD No, I haven't. I ....³ enough cable to connect up the PCs in room 510, but I ....⁴ our supplier this morning and ordered some more.

MARTIN Great. And have you connected the PCs to the printers and photocopiers?

HARALD Yes, I .... ,⁵ but there's a problem with the photocopiers.

MARTIN Can you ....⁶ it?

HARALD I don't know. I ....⁷ the software just before lunch and everything seemed OK, but Jackie rang at two and ....⁸ me she couldn't print anything from her PC to the copying machine outside her office. I ....⁹ all the connections, but they are OK. I think it's a software problem.

MARTIN Have you called the company that sold us the photocopiers?

HARALD Yes, of course. That was the first thing I .... .¹⁰

MARTIN What did they say?

HARALD They said they'd send a service technician tomorrow to have a look at it.

MARTIN OK, let's hope they can fix it. Oh, by the way, have you ....¹¹ time to see what's wrong with my laptop?

HARALD No, I .... .¹² I had a quick look at it yesterday, but I couldn't find the problem. I'll take it home with me this evening and have a look at it. It could be the hard disk. Have you backed up your files on CD recently?

MARTIN Yes, thank goodness. Thanks, Harald.

5 Complete these sentences using the Present Perfect or Past Simple of the verb in brackets.

1 ....*Have*.......... you ....*backed up*.......... all your files recently? (back up)

2 We .... some problems getting the spare parts last time. (have)

3 I .... you the drawings at the end of last week. (send)

4 How many times .... you .... fly to the USA this year? (have to)

5 We .... all the waste-water pipes last autumn. (replace)

6 .... those transistors .... , or are we still waiting for them to be delivered? (arrive)

7 .... you .... Gao Liu when you were in Shanghai? (speak to)

8 We .... never .... parts to South America before. (sold)

9 I .... to the meeting on Monday because I was visiting a customer. (not go)

10 I .... the quality report, but I'll have a look at it tomorrow. (not read)

Unit 20

1 Match the things on the left with the materials they are often made of on the right.

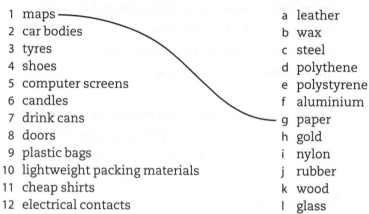

1	maps	a	leather
2	car bodies	b	wax
3	tyres	c	steel
4	shoes	d	polythene
5	computer screens	e	polystyrene
6	candles	f	aluminium
7	drink cans	g	paper
8	doors	h	gold
9	plastic bags	i	nylon
10	lightweight packing materials	j	rubber
11	cheap shirts	k	wood
12	electrical contacts	l	glass

2 Underline the properties or reasons that are correct.

1 We use gold connectors because gold
   a is strong   b <u>is a good conductor</u>   c <u>doesn't react with most chemicals</u>.

2 Plastic bags are made of polythene because it's
   a cheap   b simple to produce   c brittle.

3 Steel is used in the construction of a lot of buildings because it
   a has high tensile strength   b is ductile   c is soft.

4 A lot of cans are made of aluminium because aluminium
   a corrodes quickly   b is easy to recycle   c isn't toxic.

5 We used polystyrene in the housing of the refrigeration unit because it's
   a lightweight   b absorbent   c a good heat insulator.

6 We want to produce this part out of ceramics because ceramics
   a can withstand high temperatures   b are transparent   c are wear resistant.

7 The reason we don't use glass is because it
   a is too brittle   b can't withstand high temperatures   c is permeable.

8 We had to use platinum here because it
   a is very light   b is very ductile   c has a high melting point.

3 Complete the dialogue using the words in the list.

> brittle speeds ~~materials~~ protect
> weight nickel (x2) breaking melts
> alloys withstand high rotating

A If weight is so important, why don't you use lighter ...*materials*..[1] to build these aero-engine blades? Ceramic blades, for example.

B Yes, ...[2] is very important – but there are a lot of other factors we have to think about, too. Ceramic blades are lighter and can ....[3] high temperatures, but they are also very ....[4]

A So, if something hard was sucked into the engine and hit the blades, they would break?

B Yes.

A What about using lighter metals? Aluminium ....?[5]

B Yes, aluminium is light, but it ....[6] at about 660 °C. The temperatures inside these engines can be between 850 and 1,700 °C.

A Wow! That's hot.

B Yes, so we need to use materials that can withstand those temperatures – and don't forget the blades are ....[7] at very high ....[8]

A What does that mean?

B That means we need materials that have a very ....[9] tensile strength.

A Tensile strength?

B Yes, the materials have to be able to stretch without ....[10]

A Hmm, so what materials do you use then?

B Mainly ....[11] alloys. Look at this. This is a single-crystal ....[12] alloy turbine blade.

A But it looks as if it is made of ceramic.

B Yes, you're right, but that's because we give them a ceramic coating. The coating helps to ....[13] the blades from the high temperatures.

4 Read the dialogue in 3 again and circle T (true) or F (false).

1 Weight is the only factor in choosing materials for aero-engine blades.	T /(F)
2 Ceramic blades aren't used because they are too brittle.	T / F
3 Aluminium alloys can't be used because they are too light.	T / F
4 Aluminium alloys can't be used because they would melt in an aero-engine.	T / F
5 Tensile strength measures how far something can be pulled without breaking.	T / F
6 Pure nickel blades are normally used in aero-engines.	T / F
7 The blades are covered with a thin layer of ceramic.	T / F
8 The ceramic coating is a good conductor of heat.	T / F

5 Complete the table.

Material	is natural	is soft	is ductile	is tensile	is brittle	is / can be transparent	is a good conductor of electricity	is a good heat insulator
Gold	✔	✔	✔	✔			✔	
Glass								
Polythene								
Wood								
Steel								
Leather								
Rubber								
Paper								

6 Read this article about nanotechnology and circle T (true) or F (false).

All manufactured products are made from atoms. The properties of these products depend on how those atoms are arranged. If we rearrange or move around the atoms in coal, we can make diamonds. If we rearrange the atoms in sand (and add a few more elements), we can make computer chips. If we rearrange the atoms in dirt, water, and air, we can make potatoes.

Today's manufacturing methods are very basic and simple at the molecular level. Casting, grinding, and milling move or cut away millions of atoms. It's like trying to make things out of LEGO bricks with boxing gloves on your hands. Yes, you can push the LEGO bricks into big heaps and pile them up, but you can't put them together the way you'd like.

In the future, nanotechnology will let us take off those boxing gloves. We'll be able to snap together the basic building blocks of nature easily, inexpensively, and in lots of different ways. This will be important if we want to continue developing faster, smaller, and more powerful computer hardware. It will also let us produce completely new products that are cleaner, stronger, lighter, and more accurate.

The writer of this article thinks that ...

1 it will be possible to manufacture atoms in future.   T /Ⓕ
2 we will be able to move atoms around in the way we want.   T / F
3 it will be possible to make diamonds out of coal and potatoes out of dirt, water, and air. T / F
4 today's manufacturing methods are primitive.   T / F
5 we will probably have to wear boxing gloves if we use nanotechnology.   T / F
6 nanotechnology will allow us to produce things cheaply in future.   T / F
7 it will be possible to develop nanotechnology using faster, smaller, and more powerful
  computer hardware.   T / F
8 we will be able to produce much better products in future.   T / F

7 Read these dialogues and say how certain the second speaker is. Choose a, b, c, d, or e.

a They're certain something is possible.
b They're fairly sure something is possible.
c They don't know if it's possible or not.

d They think something is not possible.
e They're sure something is not possible.

Degree of certainty

1 A Tom, Fred asked me if it's possible to produce these parts out of aluminium.
   B Yes, that's not a problem, but we'll need more expensive cutting tools.   `a`

2 A Do you think you can repair this watch by the end of the week?
   B Probably, but it depends on what's wrong with it.

3 A Look, Manuel, we need six HB7920 pumps. Is there any way you can deliver
      them to us in the next two weeks?
   B Sorry, Pete, but there's not a hope. We don't have those pumps in stock,
      so I'll have to order them from the manufacturer.

4 A Can we deliver these parts by the end of the month?
   B I'm not sure. I'll have to check with Carlos in production planning first.

5 A Inga, do you think you can run the stress tests on these samples today?
   B Yes, sure. I'll be able to do it this afternoon.

6 A Do you think we're still going to be able to meet the deadline?
   B Hmm, probably not. We still haven't found all the bugs in the automatic
      re-ordering program.

8 Complete the dialogue with the words in the box.

| it can't be done | ~~I'm sure we can~~ | I think so | Maybe | Probably not |

A We have to find a way to reduce the weight of these electric vehicles. Do you think it's possible to
   reduce the weight of these axles?
B Yes, absolutely. *I'm sure we can* .¹ We just need to use a more expensive alloy.
A Hmm, couldn't we make the axles hollow?
B .... ² I don't think a hollow axle would have the strength we need.
A OK, can we use more plastic parts?
B .... ,³ I really don't know.
A OK, what about the batteries. Can our suppliers produce a lighter battery?
B No. I talked to them about that last week and they said ....⁴ at the moment. But the
   next generation of batteries they're developing will be smaller and more powerful.
A And when will they be available?
B In three or four months.
A Great! Do you think they'll enable us to get the range of the vehicles up to 150 km?
B Yes, ... ,⁵ but we'll have to wait and see just how powerful these new batteries are.

Unit 21

1 Read the dialogue and label the different parts of the thermoacoustic refrigeration unit.

ANNA   So, Ben, what is this machine for?

BEN   It's a thermoacoustic refrigeration unit. We developed it as an environmentally friendly alternative to a normal refrigeration unit.

ANNA   And what makes it environmentally friendly?

BEN   Well, we don't use gases such as hydrochlorofluorocarbons (HCFCs) and hydrofluorocarbons (HFCs), which are responsible for ozone depletion and global warming. We use helium – the gas you find in children's party balloons.

ANNA   OK, so how does it work?

BEN   Well, it's quite simple really. We use sound waves to generate cooling.

ANNA   So, does that mean I can keep my ice cream cool with rock music in future?

BEN   Ha! Yes, that would be nice, but we use sound waves at 173 decibels – that's many times louder than your average rock concert. You don't have to wear earplugs though, because sound levels that high can only be reached in contained, pressurized gas.

The loudspeaker at the bottom of the container moves up and down and acts as a kind of piston. When the piston rises, the pressure inside the container increases, and it compresses the helium in the inner-chamber: There's a moveable membrane at the bottom of the inner-chamber which is used to increase or decrease the pressure of the gas inside the inner-chamber. When the pressure increases, the helium shrinks in size and the temperature of the gas increases. When the pressure falls, the helium expands and the temperature falls.

ANNA   OK, I understand, but how does that help to cool a refrigerator?

BEN   Well, the key is the stack of metal screens on top of the inner-chamber. When the pressure inside the inner-chamber increases, the gas in the metal screens is compressed – it heats up, and rises.

ANNA   So, the top of the screen heats up and the lower part of the screen cools.

BEN   Exactly. We pump liquids past the lower end of the metal screens. The liquids run through pipes which go into the refrigerator and cool it.

ANNA   And what about the heat at the top end of the metal screens?

BEN   That is transferred to another tube filled with liquid. It is pumped out of the unit and is cooled by a ventilator.

ANNA   It sounds like a really cool idea, Ben.

BEN   Thanks.

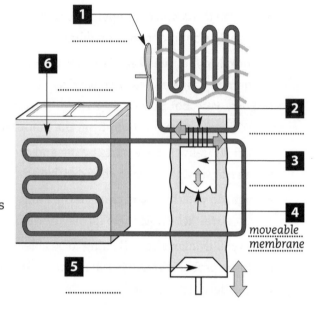

2 Read the dialogue in **1** again and circle T (true) or F (false).

1 The thermoacoustic refrigeration unit is environmentally friendlier than a normal refrigeration unit because it doesn't use gases which can cause global warming.   T /(F)

2 You can keep food and drinks cool if you store them close to loud rock music.   T / F

3 173 decibels can only be reached inside a pressurized gas container. That's why the unit isn't noisy.   T / F

4 If you reduce the pressure, the temperature of the gas increases.   T / F

5 If you increase the pressure of the gas, the gas is compressed and its temperature rises.   T / F

6 Increasing the pressure in the inner-chamber makes the gas in the metal screens hotter and causes it to rise.   T / F

7 The bottom of the metal screens is cooler which means you can cool a liquid in a pipe which goes to the refrigerator.   T / F

8 The heat at the top of the metal stacks is pumped out of the unit by a ventilator.   T / F

3 Complete the sentences using the words in the list.

because   makes   so / that's why   if   means

1 ...*If*........... you pour oil on to water, the oil floats.

2 Heating a gas, a liquid, or a solid .... it expand.

3 Water is denser than ice, but ice crystals are larger than water molecules, ... ice takes up more space.

4 Birds are not electrocuted when they sit on power lines .... they are only standing at a single point on a single line, ... electricity can't pass through it from one point to another.

5 More light .... more air pollution .... ultraviolet light turns oxygen into ozone.

6 Light travels much faster than sound .... after you see the flash of lightning it can often take several seconds before you hear the thunder.

7 Microwaves don't actually cook food, but the energy from the waves .... the water molecules vibrate at two and a half billion times a second and it is this friction that heats the food.

8 .... you put a large piece of dry ice into a glass of water, the water doesn't freeze because more heat is released by freezing a glass of water than is absorbed by vaporizing the piece of ice.

4 Here is a description of how to start a vehicle using jump leads. Number the sentences.

.... Start the engine of the other vehicle. When the engine is running, the leads are disconnected in the reverse order to that in which they were attached.

.... Then the black lead is attached to the negative terminal of the vehicle providing the jump-start. The other end of the lead should not be connected to the negative terminal of the flat battery: it should be attached a short distance away from it, such as on the engine block or on part of the vehicle's body. This reduces the risk of sparks igniting gases leaking from the battery.

.... Check that the bodies of the two vehicles are not touching before connecting the leads, otherwise a short may occur.

.... To recharge the battery, you should either go for a lengthy drive or connect the battery to a charger.

.... Start the engine of the vehicle providing the jump-start. This will prevent the good battery from discharging too.

..1.. Make sure that both batteries have the same voltage (e.g. 12V).

.... The red jump lead is used to connect the two positive terminals. First, one end of the lead is attached to the positive terminal on the flat battery and then to the positive terminal on the good battery.

5 Are these sentences from **4** active (A) or passive (P)?

1 When the engine is running, the leads are disconnected in the reverse order in that they were attached. ....P....

2 Then the black lead is attached to the negative terminal of the vehicle providing the jump-start. ....

3 This reduces the risk of sparks igniting gases leaking from the battery. ....

4 Check that the bodies of the two vehicles are not touching before connecting the leads. ....

5 You should either go for a lengthy drive or connect the battery to a charger. ....

6 Make sure that both batteries have the same voltage. ....

7 The red jump lead is used to connect the two positive terminals. ....

8 First, one end of the lead is attached to the positive terminal on the flat battery and then to the positive terminal on the good battery. ....

6 Match the beginnings of the sentences with the endings.

1 Seagulls can drink salt water

2 Paper money is not made from wood pulp, but cotton

3 If you shout for about eight and a half years,

4 Bubbles are round

5 The higher you are above the ground, the more you can see of a rainbow,

6 If you stand on your head and eat,

7 Natural gas does not have an odour

8 Water has no colour, but it reflects light. A cloudless sky

a the food still goes to your stomach.

b so some companies add a chemical to make it smell of bad eggs.

c because they have special glands which filter out the salt.

d and that's why from a plane it will appear as a complete circle.

e you will produce enough sound energy to heat a cup of coffee.

f makes it look blue.

g which means it can withstand being washed better.

h because this is the most efficient shape they can take.

Answer Key

Unit 1

1 2 g 3 b 4 f 5 a 6 h 7 e 8 c

2 2 b,c 3 b,c 4 a,b 5 a,c 6 a,b

3 2 inspect   5 maintain   8 construct
    3 equip   6 test   9 secure
    4 specify   7 produce   10 analyse

4 2 negotiating   5 maintenance   8 shipments
    3 shifts   6 troubleshoot   9 inventory
    4 inspection   7 samples   10 updating

5 2 ✓
    3 Does your company **produce** electronics?
    4 My brother **designs** safety equipment.
    5 ✓
    6 What **do** these machines do? / What does **this machine** do?
    7 ✓
    8 How long do you **keep** the records?
    9 Klaus and Pedro **provide** support to our European customers.
   10 ✓

6 2 h 3 j 4 a 5 b 6 l 7 f 8 e 9 g 10 c 11 k 12 i

7 2 Could you   5 Would you like   8 Can I
    3 Would you like   6 Can I
    4 Could you   7 Could you

Unit 2

1 2 h 3 z 4 y 5 i 6 r 7 j 8 o

2 2 Can I speak to Sarah North, please?
    3 Can I give her a message?
    4 Can you speak up?
    5 OK, go ahead.
    6 Sorry, how do you spell Vazquez?
    7 No, at E-T-C dot E-S.
    8 Is there anything else
    9 You're welcome.

3 2 g-smith1985@muc-web.de
    3 dave.hammerson@world-online.net
    4 http://www.science_world.co.uk
    5 jack.browne@essex.net

4 2 d 3 f 4 j 5 b 6 c 7 e 8 i 9 a 10 h

5 2 e 3 c 4 h 5 d 6 f 7 a 8 g

6 2 T 3 F 4 T 5 T 6 F 7 F 8 T

7 1 digital display   6 back   11 monitor
    2 dialling button   7 leg   12 keyboard
    3 wing   8 window
    4 flame   9 key
    5 arm   10 lock

8 2 a 3 f 4 g&i 5 h 6 b 7 d 8 c

9 2 numbers   6 numbers on mobile phone
    3 chair leg   7 flame
    4 door & keyboard   8 car lights
    5 key

Unit 3

1 2 c 3 h 4 e 5 g 6 d 7 b 8 a

2 2 a 3 c 4 c

3 2 will   5 won't   8 will   11 won't
    3 will   6 will   9 won't   12 will
    4 will   7 will   10 won't

4 2 How many   6 How many   10 How much
    3 How much   7 How many   11 How many
    4 How much   8 How much   12 How much
    5 How much   9 How many

5 2 How **many** weeks do you think you'll need to repair it?
    3 ✓
    4 The news **isn't** very good. It'll take about a week to get the parts we need.
    5 I think it'll cost approximately five hundred **euros** to replace.
    6 ✓
    7 ✓
    8 You're looking at something like $100,000 to buy all **this equipment**.
    9 ✓
   10 We don't have **much** time to finish this project.

6 Zap Zappy Electric Scooter
Price: €328.00   Length: 104 cm
Range: Up to 40 km   Height: Approx. 100 cm
Weight: 16.7 kg   Width: 28 cm
Battery charging time: 5 hrs   Wheels: 11-inch
Top speed: 20.8 km/h

Nissan Hypermini
Price: Approx. €30,000   Length: 266.5 cm
Range: About 115 km   Height: 155 cm
Weight: 840 kg   Width: 147.5 cm
Battery charging time: 4 hrs   Wheels: –
Top speed: 100 km/h

Estelle Comfort Electric Bicycle
Price: €1,759   Length: 195 cm
Range: Approx 27 km   Height:–
Weight: 28 kg   Width: –
Battery charging time: 2.5 hrs   Wheels: 26-inch
Top speed: 22 km/hr

7 2 T 3 F 4 F 5 F 6 T 7 F 8 T

8 Students' own answers

```
 9  ¹B U B B L E W ²R A ³P ■ ■ ⁴W
    E ■ ■ ■ ■ ■ O ■ A ■ ■ H
   ⁵T R U C K ■ ⁶R O U G H L Y
    E ■ ■ ■ ■ ■ O ■ E ■ ■ L
   ⁷E Q U I P M E N T ■ ⁹T W O
    R ■ ■ ⁸A ■ ■ ■ ¹¹V ■ I ■
    ■ ¹²C O U N T A B L E ■ ¹³D O
   ¹⁵S H I ¹⁴P ■ ¹⁶H E I G H ¹⁷T
    P ■ R ■ ■ ■ I ■ C ■ ■ O
    E ■ I ■ ■ ■ A ■ ¹⁸G A L L O N
    E ■ C ■ ■ ■ L ■ E
   ¹⁹D I M E N S I O N S
```

Unit 4

1 b electronic organizer
  c printing calculator
  d wrist camera
  e metal detector
  f laser pointer
  g remote control
  h night vision binoculars

2 2 h 3 b 4 g 5 e 6 f 7 d 8 c

3 2c, 3e, 4a, 5h, 6g, 7b, 8d

4 2 T 3 T 4 F 5 T 6 F 7 F 8 T
  9 F 10 T

5 2 pull
  3 anti-clockwise / counter-clockwise
  4 up
  5 lower
  6 on the right
  7 forwards
  8 increase

6 2 falls   5 closes   8 make
  3 turn   6 makes
  4 increase 7 use

7

Unit 5

1

2 2 had   14 had
  3 didn't know   15 was
  4 thought   16 estimated
  5 happened   17 wrote
  6 broke through 18 put
  7 poured   19 stopped
  8 tried   20 were
  9 found   21 worked
  10 had to   22 broke
  11 drilled   23 could
  12 lowered   24 started
  13 came   25 cut

3 2 F 3 T 4 T 5 F 6 F

4 2 ✓
  3 The miners didn't **know** their map was wrong.
  4 Did the rescue team know where the trapped miners **were**?
  5 They **pumped** fresh, heated air down the small hole.
  6 ✓
  7 When did the breakthrough **come**?
  8 ✓

5 2 make   5 came   8 know,
  3 see   6 give
  4 told   7 went

6 2 When was the quality circle meeting?
  3 Why did he phone Ken Thompson?
  4 What did he do / check on Wednesday morning?
  5 How many meetings did he have on Thursday?
  6 When did he go to the doctor's?
  7 Who did he have dinner with on Friday?
  8 What did he do / change on Saturday?
  9 Where did he have brunch with Sophie?
  10 Did he watch the football match?

7 Go up ↑
Energy savings
Profit
Quality
Productivity
Sales
Recycled materials
Orders
Go down ↓
Accidents
Inventory
Absenteeism
Material costs
Emissions
Downtime
Wages and salaries
Waste

8 2 to 3 to 4 by, to 5 by 6 to, by
  7 by 8 by, to

Unit 6

1 2 c 3 g 4 b 5 a 6 h 7 f 8 d

2 2 check   9 help
  3 connected   10 wrong
  4 problem   11 empty
  5 take out   12 function
  6 dry   13 manual
  7 come out   14 blocked
  8 cleaning   15 cleaned

3 2 b,c 3 b,c 4 a,b 5 a,c 6 a,b

4 2 c 3 h 4 a 5 d 6 g 7 b 8 e

5 5 HARRY I'm not sure, but it might be the cooling fan. It's …
  8 KEN I'll be right over. I'll be with you five minutes.
  1 HARRY Ken, this is Harry. What are you doing?
  9 HARRY Great! Thanks a lot, Ken.
  4 KEN What's wrong with it?
  7 HARRY How soon can you get here?
  6 KEN Yes, if it's the belt, I can …
  3 HARRY We've got a problem with one of the machines in the workshop.
  2 KEN Hello, Harry. I'm repairing …

6 2 f+j 3 g+i 4 h+o 5 b+l
6 a+k 7 e+p 8 c+m

7 2 He's drilling a hole in the ice.
3 She's cutting a tomato.
4 They're spraying a car.
5 They're repairing power lines.
6 She's running a test.
7 They're constructing a building.
8 She's filling up a car with petrol.

Unit 7

1 2 Where   6 What   10 What
3 Which   7 Why   11 Where
4 How   8 When   12 Which
5 Who   9 Who

2 2 long   5 colour   8 often
3 kind of   6 many
4 much   7 size

3 2 take   5 take   8 take
3 last   6 took
4 last   7 last

4 2 in 3 in 4 on 5 on 6 at 7 on
8 in 9 at 10 at

5 2 1,000,000,000   6 100,000 m³
3 1,000,000 m²   7 100,000,000
4 1,000,000,000,000   8 1.999
5 1999

6 2 c 3 b 4 a 5 b 6 c 7 c 8 c

7 2 hundreds of thousands
3 75,000 years
4 4,000 km
5 35 cm
6 75%
7 21°
8 85 km x 45 km
9 74 cm higher
10 600,000 years
11 50 km
12 1,000 km
13 1,000 km³
14 12.5 cm
15 a few thousand
16 billions

Unit 8

1 2 T 3 F 4 T 5 F 6 F 7 T 8 T

2 2 have to   7 don't have to
3 mustn't   8 mustn't
4 must   9 have to
5 mustn't   10 needn't
6 mustn't

3 2 c 3 d 4 b 5 c 6 a 7 b 8 d

4 2 d 3 b 4 a 5 c 6 a

5 1 handlebars   7 dynamo
2 screen   8 rollers
3 electric wire   9 cam
4 remote control unit   10 gears

5 book holder   11 support
6 on/off switch   12 saddle

6 2 F 3 T 4 T 5 F 6 T 7 F 8 T

7 2 a,b,d   5 a,b,c   8 a,c,d
3 b,c,d   6 a,b,c   9 a,b,d
4 a,b,c   7 b,c,d   10 b,c,d

8 2 F 3 F 4 T 5 F 6 T

Unit 9

1 2 h 3 b 4 a 5 c 6 e 7 f 8 d

2 2 could   8 shouldn't
3 could   9 should
4 should   10 could
5 should   11 should
6 shouldn't   12 should
7 could

3 2 c 3 h 4 b 5 g 6 j 7 f 8 a
9 d 10 i

4 b 7 c 5 d 9 e 1 f 8

5 2 F 3 F 4 T 5 T 6 T 7 F 8 F

6 2 tightly   6 easily
3 well   7 fast
4 slowly   8 completely
5 hard

7 2 badly   6 slowly
3 fast   7 easily
4 hard   8 completely
5 well

8 2 good   6 easily
3 physically   7 gentle
4 solid   8 easy, carefully,
5 serious   properly

Unit 10

1 2 triangle   7 cone
3 oval   8 sphere
4 cylinder   9 square
5 semi-circle   10 rectangle
6 circle

2 2 semi-circle   7 spherical
3 square   8 cube
4 triangular   9 rectangular
5 cylinder   10 oval
6 conical

3 2 U-shaped
3 L-shaped
4 star-shaped
5 Y-shaped
6 X-shaped
7 T-shaped
8 S-shaped

4 See diagram on page 80.

5 2 b 3 c 4 a 5 d 6 c 7 a 8 b

6 Colours   Shapes
purple   sphere
pink   cube
yellow   rectangle
green   cone
oval
Materials   cylinder
steel
plastic   **Tools/Machines**
copper   scissors
titanium   wrench
cotton   calculator
rubber   saw
aluminium   control unit
quartz   pump

7 See crossword on page 80.

Unit 11

1 2 T 3 F 4 F 5 F 6 T 7 T 8 T

2 2 A 3 P 4 A 5 P 6 A 7 A 8 P

3 2 is written   4 are given
3 are done   5 is made

4 2 Use this   6 It has
3 It has   7 It's for
4 It's for   8 This keeps
5 Rotate

5 2 b 3 a 4 b 5 c 6 d 7 a,b 8 c

6 2 c 3 a 4 b 5 g 6 e 7 f 8 d

7

Unit 12

1 2 f 3 h 4 a 5 d 6 c 7 e 8 g

2 2 h 3 e 4 f 5 g 6 a 7 c 8 b

3 2 e 3 a 4 j 5 b 6 c 7 h 8 d
9 f 10 g

4 2 for drying
3 actually behind you
4 are sharp
5 cancer in laboratory mice
6 For indoor
7 will be prosecuted
8 Warning: misuse may

5 2 a 3 g 4 c 5 b 6 d 7 h 8 e

6 2 T 3 F 4 T 5 T 6 F 7 T 8 F 9 F
10 T

7 Making a suggestion
What we need are
Why don't we
I think we should
Couldn't we
how about
Agreeing
I think it's a great idea
Exactly!
That's a good idea
Yes, you're right
Yes, that's not a bad idea
Yes, why not
Disagreeing
They're too expensive
Yes, but
Perhaps, but
Maybe, but
That's crazy

Unit 13

1 2 through   5 over
3 around   6 between
4 past   7 under

2 2 under   5 through
3 along   6 over
4 past   7 between

3 2 F 3 F 4 T 5 F

4 2 along   9 take
3 turn   10 side
4 between   11 along
5 through   12 river
6 come   13 (railway) bridge
7 roundabout   14 left
8 roundabout   15 follow

5 2 car hire   9 restaurant
company   10 airport
3 airport   11 restaurant
4 restaurant   12 car hire
5 car hire   company
company   13 airport
6 car hire   14 car hire
company   company
7 airport   15 restaurant
8 airport

6 2 list   7 bill
3 Here you are   8 Can I pay
4 order   9 make it
5 I'd like some   10 receipt
6 how would   11 a mistake
you like   12 bring

7 2 Has anyone given you anything to
carry?
3 Have you had this bag with you the
whole time?
4 Are you carrying any knives or

sharp instruments?
5 Do you have any electrical items
with you?
6 Can I see your boarding card and
passport?
7 Put all the metal objects in your
pockets in this tray.
8 Open that bag and take out all the
electrical items in it.

8 2 No, they haven't. 5 No, I don't
3 Yes, I have. 6 Of course.
4 No, I'm not. Here you are.

Unit 14

1 2 5   8 150,000 tonnes
3 55 km/h   9 1,250
4 6 days   10 18m²
5 2004   11 137m²
6 345m   12 16 km
7 72m

2 72 m, 345 m, 18 m², 137 m²

3 2 $800,000,000
3 2004
4 5; 1,250
5 150,000 tonnes
6 6 days

4 2 length   4 weight   6 depth
3 wide   5 old   7 fast

5 2 old   4 fast   6 long
3 wide   5 deep   7 heavy

6 2 high   5 high   7 high
3 tall   6 tall   8 tall
4 high

7 2 is   5 isn't   8 are
3 isn't   6 aren't   9 isn't
4 isn't   7 are

8 2 a few   5 much   8 a few
3 many   6 a little   9 a little
4 many   7 much   10 many

9 2 c 3 h 4 f 5 a 6 g 7 e 8 b

Unit 15

1 2 free   8 check
3 schedule   9 to confirm
4 tied up   10 a note
5 take   11 need
6 How about   12 by
7 say

2 2 until   6 by   10 by
3 until   7 by   11 until
4 by   8 by
5 until   9 until

3 2 g 3 b 4 f 5 a 6 c 7 d 8 h

4 Suggesting a time
Are you free on Friday?
Shall we say six-thirty?

How about 12.30?
Saying 'Yes'
Wednesday at 10 is fine.
That's good for me.
Yes, I'm free then.

Saying 'No'
I'm afraid I'm busy then.
I can't make 8.30, I'm afraid.
No, I'm afraid I can't manage Tuesday.

Saying when you are available
I can't make ten, but I can manage
eleven.
I won't be back until 2.30.
I'm tied up most of this week, but
next week's better.

Estimating time
Half an hour should be long enough.
How long do we need?
How long do you think it'll take?

Confirming arrangements
I'll talk to Sue and confirm it later.
OK, I'll meet you there at nine o'clock.
OK, let's say three-thirty in your
office, then.

5 2 T 3 F 4 F 5 F 6 T 7 F
8 T 9 T

6 2 I'm afraid that
3 Please get back to me
4 We are sorry about
5 Please could you
6 Yours sincerely
7 Sorry
8 Do you want me to
9 Thank you for
10 We would be happy to
11 Please confirm
12 Looking forward to

7 2 e 3 b 4 d 5 c 6 a 7 b 8 d
9 f 10 c 11 a 12 e 13 b 14 d

8 2 (Please) Could you / Can you / I'd
appreciate it if you could
3 I'm afraid
4 Looking forward to / We look
forward to
5 Thanks for / Thank you for
6 I'm afraid
7 (Please) Could you / Can you / I'd
appreciate it if you could
8 We would be pleased / happy to
9 I am attaching
10 Looking forward to / We look
forward to

Unit 16

1 2 b 3 a 4 b 5 a

2 2 f 3 g 4 h 5 c 6 e 7 b 8 a

3 2 competitive market

3 lead times
4 Just-in-time production
5 finished goods
6 supply chain
7 retail outlets
8 product cycle times

4 1 inspection   5 melting
   2 washing   6 filtering
   3 flotation tank   7 pelletizing
   4 drying

5 2 f   3 g   4 a   5 e   6 b   7 c

6 2 blow up   5 sort out
   3 cut up   6 heat up
   4 take apart   7 throw away

7 2 take out   5 blow up
   3 take apart   6 sort out
   4 throw away   7 heat up

8 See crossword on page 80.

Unit 17

1 1 j   2 g   3 c   4 b   5 k   6 a   7 h   8 f
  9 e   10 l   11 d   12 i

2 2 turns   10 pulls
   3 is connected to   11 is supported by
   4 are hinged   12 is held in place
   5 are attached to   13 downwards
   6 clockwise   14 rises
   7 drops   15 inspect
   8 move   16 wear
   9 fall

3 2 F   3 T   4 T   5 F   6 F   7 F   8 T
  9 T   10 T

4 2 c   3 a   4 b   5 a   6 c   7 b   8 c

5 1 dust cap   5 cup
   2 bolt   6 cone
   3 washer   7 spindle
   4 crank   8 chain ring

6 2 F   3 T   4 F   5 T   6 T   7 F   8 T
  9 F   10 T

7 2 in front of
   3 under
   4 above
   5 on the front of
   6 on the back of
   7 on the bottom of
   8 behind

Unit 18

1 2 T   3 F   4 T   5 F   6 T   7 T   8 F

2 2 safer
   3 better
   4 more clearly
   5 faster
   6 earlier
   7 better
   8 more carefully
   9 more expensive, higher
  10 heavier
  11 more cheaply
  12 faster

3 2 are you sure
   3 Why don't we
   4 can't afford that
   5 the hold-up
   6 not ready yet
   7 speed them up
   8 don't forget
   9 are we going to do
  10 nothing else
  11 long enough
  12 It should be
  13 won't that be
  14 to solve
  15 go out of
  16 a big risk to take

4 1 C   2 A   3 B

5 2 M   3 T   4 Q   5 T   6 M   7 T   8 Q

6 2 won't meet, fix
   3 'll install, buy
   4 need, 'll send
   5 'll have, doesn't improve
   6 'll send, can't

7 2 e   3 a   4 g   5 b   6 h   7 d   8 f

8 See crossword on page 80.

Unit 19

1 2 was asked   7 was stopped
   3 was built   8 was designed
   4 was given   9 was done
   5 was needed   10 wasn't built
   6 was given   11 was constructed

2 2 F   3 T   4 T   5 F   6 T   7 T   8 F

3 2 When was it built?
   3 Who was the first personal
     computer produced by?
   4 How much memory was it
     equipped with?
   5 Who was the first pocket
     calculator invented by?
   6 Where was it produced?
   7 What was the first TV remote
     control unit called?
   8 When was it produced?

4 2 came   8 told
   3 didn't have   9 've checked
   4 called   10 did
   5 have   11 had
   6 fix   12 haven't
   7 installed

5 2 had   7 Did, speak
   3 sent   8 have, sold
   4 have, had to   9 didn't go
   5 replaced   10 haven't read
   6 Have, arrived

Unit 20

1 2 c   3 j   4 a   5 l   6 b   7 f   8 k   9 d   10 e   11 i
  12 h

2 2 a, b   3 a, b   4 b, c   5 a, c   6 a, c   7 a, b
   8 b, c

3 2 weight   6 melts   10 breaking
   3 withstand   7 rotating   11 nickel
   4 brittle   8 speeds   12 nickel
   5 alloys   9 high   13 protect

4 2 T   3 F   4 T   5 T   6 F   7 T   8 F

5 See table on page 80.

6 2 T   3 T   4 T   5 F   6 T   7 F   8 T

7 2 b   3 e   4 c   5 a   6 d

8 2 Probably not.
   3 Maybe
   4 it can't be done
   5 I think so

Unit 21

1 1 ventilator
   2 stack of metal screens
   3 inner-chamber
   4 moveable membrane
   5 loudspeaker / piston
   6 refrigerator

2 2 F   3 T   4 F   5 T   6 T   7 T   8 F

3 2 makes   5 means, because
   3 so / that's why   6 so / that's why
   4 because, so,   7 makes
     that's why   8 if

4 6 Start the engine of the other
     vehicle …
   4 Then the black lead is attached to …
   2 Check that the bodies of the two
     vehicles are …
   7 To recharge the battery, you should …
   5 Start the engine of the vehicle …
   1 Make sure that both batteries …
   3 The red jump lead is used to …

5 2 P   3 A   4 A   5 A   6 A   7 P   8 P

6 2 g   3 e   4 h   5 d   6 a   7 b   8 f

Answers

Unit 10 Ex 4

Unit 10 Ex 7

Unit 16 Ex 8

Unit 18 Ex 7

Material	is natural	is soft	is ductile	is tensile	is brittle	is/can be transparent	is a good conductor of electricity	is a good heat insulator
Gold	✔	✔	✔	✔			✔	
Glass					✔	✔		✔
Polythene		✔	✔	✔		✔		✔
Wood	✔		✔	✔				
Steel			✔	✔			✔	
Leather	✔	✔	✔	✔				✔
Rubber	✔	✔	✔	✔				✔
Paper	✔	✔	✔					✔

Unit 20 Ex 5